URBAN
STREETSCAPES
A WORKBOOK FOR DESIGNER

URBAN STREETSCAPES

A WORKBOOK FOR DESIGNERS

Johanna Gibbons & Bernard Oberholzer

LAYOUT & ILLUSTRATIONS BY
Johanna Gibbons & Terry Milne

OXFORD
BSP PROFESSIONAL BOOKS
LONDON EDINBURGH BOSTON
MELBOURNE PARIS BERLIN VIENNA

BSP Professional Books
A division of Blackwell Scientific
  Publications Ltd
Editorial offices:
Osney Mead, Oxford OX2 0EL
25 John Street, London WC1N 2BL
23 Ainslie Place, Edinburgh EH3 6AJ
3 Cambridge Center, Cambridge,
  MA 02142, USA
54 University Street, Carlton,
  Victoria 3053, Australia

First published 1991

Set by Best-set Typesetter Ltd. Hong Kong
Printed and bound in Great Britain by
The University Press, Cambridge.

DISTRIBUTORS

Marston Book Services Ltd
PO Box 87
Oxford OX2 0DT
(*Orders:* Tel: 0865 791155
         Fax: 0865 791927
         Telex: 837515)

USA
  Blackwell Scientific Publications, Inc.
  3 Cambridge Center
  Cambridge, MA 02142
  (*Orders:* Tel: (800) 759-6102)

Canada
  Oxford University Press
  70 Wynford Drive
  Don Mills
  Ontario M3C 1J9
  (*Orders:* Tel: (416) 441-2941)

Australia
  Blackwell Scientific Publications
  (Australia) Pty Ltd
  54 University Street
  Carlton, Victoria 3053
  (*Orders:* Tel: (03) 347-0300)

British Library
Cataloguing in Publication Data

Gibbons, Johanna
  Urban streetscapes: a workbook for designers.
  I. Title   II. Oberholzer, Bernard
  711.4
  ISBN 0-632-02323-6

Contents

Acknowledgements

We wish to thank the following people for their contribution to the book:

Anthony Blee, Luke Gibbons and Terry Milne for their valued professional advice and editing skills, and most important of all, for their continuous support and enthusiasm during the lengthy production of the book.

Henry Aikman for line drawings on the following pages: l 20, 23, 25, 27, l 30, c 58, l 71, c and l 133, c 134, c 148, c 151.

Jenny Lovell for her general assistance.

Julia Burden, Commissioning Editor, for being so very patient and backing the initial idea.

Hulton Picture Company for permission to reproduce the black and white photograph of Piccadilly Circus 1899 on page 2.

We acknowledge: OVP Associates, Waterfront Landscape Architects, Victoria & Alfred Waterfront Company, Durban City Engineer's Department, Cape Town City Planning Department, Port Elizabeth City Engineer's Department, Ciskei Directorate of Planning, Revel Fox who provided guidance on the Durban and St George's Mall Street furniture, and Peter Dijkhuis who participated in the development of the Victoria and Alfred Street furniture system.

The following manufacturers are credited whose products are traced in Section 2 to accompany the text on the following pages: Abacus Municipal Ltd u 97; Architen Ltd l 161 and l 162; Ballentine Boness Iron Co Ltd u 12 and u r 98; Barton Corporation c 10; Bega c 126; Britannia Architectural Metalwork and Restoration Ltd c 97; British Gates and Timber Ltd l 97; CAM Architectural Metalwork c 98; Country Forge Ltd u l 98; Dorothea Ltd c and l 43, u 44, u 52, u l 79, c and l 87, u 120 and 144; ECC Quarries c l 28; Edenhall Concrete Products Ltd 29; Enkamat 10; Erlau and AG Park Furniture c r 53 and l 54; Glynwed Brickhouse l 11; Haws Drinking Fawcet Company 178; Ibstock Building Products Ltd l 110 and l 111; KeeKlamp u 97; Lister u 53 and l 68; Macemain Engineering Ltd c 160 and l left 98; Machin u 161; Marley Paving Co l 9; Marshalls Mono Ltd l 9, c 10, u 43, c 68, 70, l r 98; Mawrob Co Ltd l 98; Milner Delvaux Ltd c 8, l 34; MMG Engineering Ltd u 110; Neenah Foundry Company l 42; Period Ironmongery Ltd l 120; Pinex Timber Products Ltd u 111; Se'lux u 142 and l 144; Singer & James Ltd l 96; Staff l 126; Stapeley Water Gardens l 176, u 177; Steetley Concrete Products c r 28; Sternberg 127; Streetscene c 79, u 96; Townart l 52; Townscape Ltd c l 53, u 69, l 79, 86, u 87 and c 97; Woodhouse l 53, u 54, u r 79 and 143; Zephyr Flags & Banners 145.

Photographs were taken by Johanna & Luke Gibbons and Bernard Oberholzer. All photographs were taken Fujichrome film and converted to black and white for the purposes of this publication.

Introduction

Buildings might be designed by architects, and roads by civil engineers, while the no-man's land in between is still an area of confused design responsibility. Yet it is the design of urban spaces , with all their facilities and equipment, that provide the setting for the life and activities of the city.

A new consciousness about urban spaces has evolved in the last few decades. The spate of books and schemes dealing with pedestrianisation and streetscape improvement is evidence of this interest. There has been a revival in the use of the street as a space for life in the community, and not just a channel for vehicular movement. This may be seen as a return in some respects to the way streets were used before cars dominated the scene.

The importance of well designed streetscape elements, which give a street its own particular character, is being rediscovered. Ultimately, it is this ubiquitous hardware which can either enhance or detract from the quality of our streets.

The design of street furniture has generally been a neglected field, a vacuum that many, including landscape architects, have recently sought to fill. It is regrettable that industrial designers have not played a more significant role in this area.

The authors have felt for some time a need for a source-book of good ideas on street furniture that could perhaps sharpen the awareness and widen the present scope of design thinking. The purpose of this book is therefore not to devise standards for street furniture, which would only lead to more uniformity, but rather to explore the potential and some of the ingredients of their design.

Firstly, basic principles for each type of streetscape element are given, so that some of the more obvious problems and pitfalls may be avoided by those who venture into street furniture design. These deal with the practicalities of function, materials, selection and siting. The principles are then followed by examples of design responses in particular situations for each element, the examples being drawn from many different contexts, cultures and even periods.

Some of the examples may not seem to be applicable in present-day terms, but they are included because of their contribution to the character of the streetscape or townscape. The selection of examples was the result of a personal search by the authors not only for good design, but also for other qualities such as appropriateness, spontaneity, durability and timelessness.

The compilation of this work-book may be seen as the identification of that elusive quality that Gordon Cullen alluded to as 'the art of the environment', and that Christopher Alexander refers to as 'the quality without a name', with reference to the wider context of townscape and building.

The sources of the material for the book come from extensive observation by each of the authors in Europe, North America, the Far East, Australia and Southern Africa. In addition, material has been drawn from journals and trade literature, as well as from the authors' own projects.

The designer is encouraged to extend the range of ideas illustrated on these pages by starting his own scrapbook on streetscape design, and invited to propose these ideas and observations to the authors for inclusion into a more comprehensive work-book in the future. Perhaps in this way many good ideas will be shared, and even refined, instead of lying fallow on dusty shelves, or being forgotten altogether.

Section 1

ISSUES IN STREETSCAPE DESIGN

Issues in Streetscape Design

STREET FURNITURE IN PERSPECTIVE

Piccadilly Circus, London, 1899

The contemporary street scene with its clutter of hardware, is a relatively recent phenomenon. If you look at old photographs of any city, you may see a few lamp-posts, the odd park bench, a drinking fountain and modest signage on the ground floor facade. Sometimes overhead wires for trams dangled above the main routes.

Gradually, various utilities, clinical street lighting and parking meters made their appearance, together with an inundation of signage and advertising competing for attention. Plastic wrappings, fast food and the 'throw-away' culture brought with it a proliferation of litter bins.

At first these new street furniture elements were designed in an uncoordinated manner, aggravated by the variety of new materials that became available. But with the advent of urban revitalisation projects, such as pedestrian malls, 'woonerven' (3 m wide carriageways in shared vehicular-pedestrian streets), waterfronts and historic precincts, there has been greater focus on the importance of the design of the streetscape, including paving and street furniture.

IDENTITY IN STREETSCAPE AND TOWNSCAPE

With the growth of cities and suburbs, came a tendency towards relentless uniformity in the streetscape, so that often there may be little difference in character between the various districts of the city, or even from one country to another. Yet the most enjoyable and memorable cities are those which have a sense of place, and where well-defined precincts or districts each have their own particular atmosphere.

This may have prompted planners such as Kevin Lynch in the United States, for example, to attempt to identify and then reinforce the particular uniqueness of a district through urban design measures. This approach has been carried further in the restoration of historic areas, for the development of district themes for residental projects, office parks, campuses and expo' sites.

Development of such themes would normally take into account the context, such as an urban square or waterfront, the regional architecture, and the activities and needs of the users. Techniques usually involve the use of a particular design vocabulary, consistent use of materials and detailing, and the coordination of signage, graphics and colours.

Street furniture used to articulate and define spaces

Seen in this way street furniture can contribute to the identity of a place and to the making or improvement of urban spaces. For example a focus can be created with the use of a water feature, while entrances, routes and edges can be defined by the strategic placement of lamp standards, bollards and trees.

Urban revitalisation projects, whether large or small, in the form of pedestrianisation and sidewalk widening schemes, provide opportunities for the comprehensive re-design of the street furniture. The improvement of paving and street furniture can in turn have a chain reaction on surrounding properties, providing an incentive for people to upgrade their own building and take pride in their environment.

DESIGN CONSIDERATIONS

Haphazard assemblage of traffic hardware

Traditionally the selection and placing of individual street furniture items has been in the hands of engineers and treated on an *ad hoc* basis, with the result that no coherence or design theme is usually evident. The items are often selected for their initial low cost, rather than appropriateness, durability and aesthetic merit, reflecting an expedient attitude, rather than a considered design approach with attention given to detail.

At the other extreme, one often sees futile and ridiculous attempts to mimic antique street furniture elements, such as gas lanterns using high-pressure sodium fittings. This may have relevance in certain restoration work where authentic detailing is required, but not when applied in contemporary street environments. A few lighting manufacturers, notably those in Germany, have managed to produce elegant light fittings which blend comfortably into both old and new parts of a city.

Another problem is the tendency to over-design the streetscape, creating stage sets which feel unreal or have a Disneyland quality. Good street furniture, like good buildings, should be more spontaneous, and look as if it has always belonged to the street.

Bath, England ● simplicity and elegance

Designers and manufacturers, in their infatuation with new synthetic materials, such as plastics, often overlook the advantages of natural materials which are more subtle in colour and texture, feel more alive to the touch, and which can even improve with age and weathering, while their synthetic counterparts can only deteriorate. One can draw much inspiration from the Japanese in the way they use natural materials such as wood, bamboo, stone and gravel.

In the design of a 'family' of street furniture elements, it is usually safer to limit the range of materials used, as well as the fixing details. One is sometimes struck by the simplicity and elegance of an old Victorian streetscape, where the lamp-posts, signage, railings and benches are all made from moulded cast-iron components, usually taken from a catalogue and often produced at the local foundry.

In certain areas with severe climatic conditions, the selection of materials may be critical, such as beachfronts, where the materials need to withstand corrosion from salt-spray, or damage from wind-loading.

COORDINATED STREET FURNITURE

Un-coordinated array of elements

Because individual street furniture items tend to be the responsibility of different departments, or even authorities, they are usually installed as independent systems, resulting in an uncoordinated array of elements and poles. The problem is not only the variety of elements, but the way in which they are distributed in the street.

It is important therefore that in the first place the cooperation of the various departments is obtained, in order that the number and type of elements and poles can be rationalised. A reasonable approach would be to create a 'family' of street furniture elements, in which each element such as a sign, litter bin or light fitting would have a similar fixing detail and a common support pole.

One project, in which the authors participated, makes use of only a few ingredients; a tubular metal pole of standard diameter and a common fixing collar, as well as a colour theme and special logo for each district of the city.

Coordinated elements with standardised fixing collars

These pole supports and fixing collars were shared by the many city departments responsible for street lighting, street names, traffic signs and litter bins, where previously each department had used its own pole and clamping detail, along with a myriad colours and materials. This standardisation helps not only to visually unify the wide range of street furniture elements, but also to facilitate installation, as well as modification, addition and replacement of elements.

One of the greatest benefits of a coordinated street furniture system, is that the various elements can also be grouped more easily. A bus shelter or kiosk could for example become a support for other elements such as lighting, signs, advertisements, benches or telephones.

AN INTEGRATED APPROACH

An integrated approach

We have tried to stress the attitude that the design of street furniture should not be seen as an end in itself, but something that forms part of the broader streetscape and townscape. The street furniture theme should ideally form part of an overall urban design concept, that gives coherence and legibility to the city.

We have also argued that individual street furniture elements should not be seen in isolation, but rather as part of a coordinated street furniture system, where all the elements are considered together and properly related to surrounding buildings. In the design of even the smallest element therefore, the vision of the whole should not be lost. Examples of this coordinated approach are illustrated in Section 3 of the book.

Section 2
GENERAL PRINCIPLES

Paving
Manhole Covers

Paving
Manhole Covers

PAVING

DESIGN CONCEPT

A consistent layout of paving materials and patterns can contribute a significant unifying effect to the streetscape and provide a distinctive identity for a village, town or city. Paving can also give a sense of continuity between different areas, particularly where a single material is used for edges and channels.

PAVING THEMES

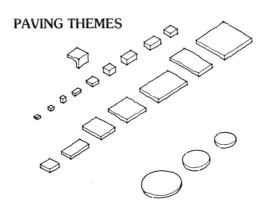

Paving can be considered as a neutral backdrop, or alternatively, can be more ornate to attract attention, create a focus or festive atmosphere, or provide a 'rug' for an important circulation node or doorway. Carefully coordinated changes in colour and texture help to provide contrast, richness and a sense of scale.

A vocabulary of materials and colours should be selected, so that these reflect the qualities particular to a place. Using this palette, different themes may be chosen for each precinct or street.

SELECTION

Traditional paving themes were based on tried and tested indigenous materials and patterns and these should be recognised. The re-use of old paving materials and the mixing of old and new can give newly paved areas an instantly established look.

The following aspects should be considered when selecting materials:

- *Use*: pedestrian, vehicular traffic, desire lines, deterrents.
- *Application*: formal, informal, public, private, corporate.
- *Cost*: material, laying, maintenance and/or replacement cost.
- *Strength*: pedestrian loading, light and heavy vehicular loading.
- *Bonding*: visual, practical, and structural considerations.
- *Maintenance*: durability, ease of cleaning and repairing.
- *Jointing*: colour, width and type of jointing material.
- *Construction*: rigid or flexible, loading capabilities.
- *Pre-cast v. in situ material*: quality of workmanship, site specific requirements.
- *Appropriateness*: origin of material, suitability in relation to the architectural and/or regional context.

GENERAL PRINCIPLES

PAVING TEXTURE

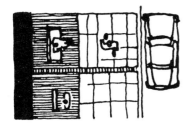

Surface texture can respond to the type of pedestrian movement:

- Textured surfaces for stationary pedestrians where benches or information boards occur.
- Even surfaces for moving pedestrians along desire lines and sidewalks.

Textured paving, such as exposed aggregate, ribbed concrete or other non-slip surfaces are recommended on ramps, around water features and other hazards such as quaysides. A dimpled texture is highly recommended to assist blind people, on dropped kerbs and at pedestrian crossings.

Rough paving such as cobbles or riverstones can be used to deter pedestrians or slow down vehicles.

PAVING PATTERNS

Large areas can be articulated by using bricks or cobbles for banding, edging and infill panels.

Special areas or circulation nodes can be emphasised by:

- A break in paving rhythm.
- The introduction of a 'special paver'.
- The insertion of a special feature such as a city logo.

Patterning could respond to the formal or informal nature of an area, for example:

- Simple, formal treatment for historic areas.
- Informal or colourful treatment for beachfronts.

and also to the scale of the spaces, for example:

- Bold treatment: large plazas, squares or formal promenades.
- Fine-grain treatment: lanes, narrow pedestrian streets and courtyards.

BONDING

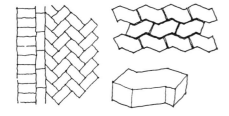

Interlocking units, termed *flexible paving*, or the use of herringbone bond, are preferable where large areas of brick or block paving are to be laid and trafficked. The interlocking bond is able to resist the braking actions and turning movements of vehicles.

Basket weave, running bond and stack bond offer continuous straight lines and are more susceptible to paving failure under loading. These bond patterns should be limited to pedestrian areas only.

It is preferable to lay bricks or slabs in staggered bond since straight lines are difficult to achieve practically in large areas.

COLOUR

The effect of colour should be considered when selecting materials.

- Light colours will reflect light and cause glare.
- Dark colours absorb heat and may suffer from thermal movement.
- Mottled, dark colours can camouflage oil slicks and general staining.

Colour fade of pigmented blocks should be anticipated, whereas the natural colour of stone and clay is predictable and improves with weathering. Contrasts in paving colours should be sufficiently pronounced to read well despite normal wear and tear.

EYE LEVEL

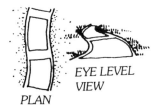

PLAN   EYE LEVEL VIEW

Foreshortening, when viewed in perspective, exaggerates curves and reduces the width of bands and panels.

Generous radii should be used so that at eye level comfortable curvilinear patterns can be perceived.

A minimum width for banding (say 900 mm) across the vanishing plane can help to offset the effect of foreshortening.

REINFORCED GRASS

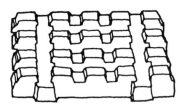

In natural or recreational areas where grass is more appropriate, it may be necessary to reinforce the grass for uses such as:

- One-day markets.
- Temporary parking.
- Emergency or service access.
- Rural aircraft runways.

Reinforcing can be achieved with special concrete perforated slabs, bricks with open joints, synthetic matting, cellular plastic sheets or a 'sandwich' construction using grass sods in conjunction with layers of gravel or hoggin reinforced with various plastic meshes.

POROSITY

Where trees are planted into paving the porosity of the paving material should be considered. Gravel, for instance, would allow water and air to reach tree roots, while tarmac and concrete usually form an impervious surface.

If impervious materials are selected, openings a minimum of 1 m square should be allowed around a tree. These can be covered with a tree grid to maintain paving continuity.

Generally water is more useful to trees if it is drained through the soil rather than collected in a sewer, and therefore more porous paving surfaces are desirable. Other benefits from drainage into the ground can be reduced stormwater and irrigation requirements.

DRAINAGE

Paving should be designed with cross-falls to act as a self-cleaning mechanism. Channels can be incorporated into the edge patterning to take away surface water. Recommended falls vary with the material selected but generally range between 1:40 and 1:80.

If water is allowed to lie on paving, discoloration and slippery surfaces result.

The surface drainage arrangements should be designed to avoid visible valleys and high points which create awkward undulations.

CONSTRUCTION

Construction considerations include the following:

- *Sub-base*: specifications depend on ground conditions and anticipated loading.
- *Bedding*: specifications depend on whether a flexible or rigid pavement is being used.
- *Expansion joints*: their recommended frequency depend on climatic conditions and materials.
- *Edge restraints*: to hold the paving firmly in place include kerbs and channels or a combination of the two.

MANHOLE COVERS

DISUSED MANHOLES

Abandoned manholes should be sealed off and filled in. Covers should be removed and the area repaved.

POSITION

Where possible the position of manhole covers should be integrated into the paving pattern and aligned with buildings, so that brick and slab cutting can be kept to a minimum.

RECESSED

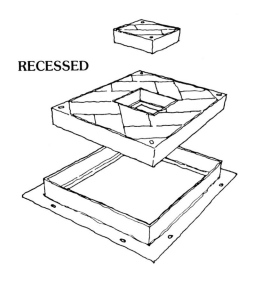

Manhole covers can be recessed to receive brick pavers, or other matching material, for continuity of paving. Lifting bosses should be robust and vandal-proof as the filled covers will weigh considerably more than standard ones.

Some covers are designed with reinforcing bars and solid or open bases to receive *in situ* concrete or asphalt. These are also suitable for tile infill, and can be adapted for heavy-duty or pedestrian use.

MATERIALS

Materials may be either ductile cast iron or steel. Steel covers are designed for areas where vehicular speed and concentration is restricted to a minimum. Cast-iron covers can be used for heavy-duty use and have the advantage of allowing the city crest or any other logo to be incorporated in the design.

SKID RESISTANCE AND ANTI-ROCKING

A skid resistant texture is preferable, incorporated into the surface pattern. Non-rocking devices consist of a three point suspension to the cover and machine seating.

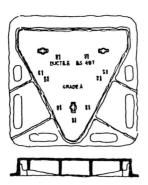

ACROPOLIS · ATHENS · GREECE
· DESIGN : DEMITRIS PIKIONIS 1951 - 1957
· RICH AND SYMPATHETIC PAVING DETAIL
  USING A FREEFORM PATTERN OF TILES ·
  STONE SLABS AND COBBLES

TOFUKUJI · KYOTO · JAPAN
IMMACULATELY RAKED GRAVEL
STONE EDGING AND CHANNEL / DRAIN

RYE · ENGLAND
· TRADITIONAL PAVING MATERIALS
· STONE PAVING SLABS AND ROAD STONES
WITH ROUNDED RIVER COBBLES

TSUKUBA , NEAR TOKYO , JAPAN
, STRIKING COMBINATION OF DIFFERENT
SIZED AND COLOURED GRIDS OVERLAPPED
USING GLAZED TILES

REGENT HOTEL , HONG KONG
, GRID PAVING DESIGN USING ONE
MATERIAL WITH TWO DIFFERENT
FINISHES — FLAMED AND POLISHED

DAITOKUJI · KYOTO · JAPAN
· STEPPING STONES IN ANGULAR GRAVEL
CONNECTING STONE PAVED AREAS

SAN FRANCISCO · USA
· GEOMETRIC PAVING EDGE
· STEPPING STONES PROVIDE A VISUAL
TRANSITION BETWEEN PAVING AND TURF

GENERAL PRINCIPLES

TOKYO ' JAPAN
' SIMPLE USE OF CHARCOAL AND RED SMOOTH
BRICKS IN HERRINGBONE PATTERN TO
GREAT EFFECT
' GIVES THE IMPRESSION OF RAKED GRAVEL

SAN FRANCISCO · USA
· GRASSCRETE USED AS A TRANSITION
BETWEEN IN SITU CONCRETE PAVING
AND TURF

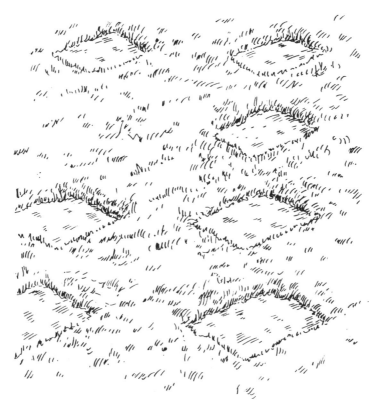

TOFUKUJI · KYOTO · JAPAN
· SQUARE STONE SLABS SET ON THE
DIAGONAL INTO MOSSY GROUND COVER
· THEY FORM A PATTERN OF STEPPING STONES

DAITOKUJI · KYOTO · JAPAN
· STONE SLABS AND COBBLES FORM A PATH
THROUGH GRAVEL PAVING

MILAN · ITALY
· STONE COBBLES AND SLABS
· VEHICULAR ROUTE DEFINED THROUGH A
PEDESTRIAN ZONE

TOFUKUJI · KYOTO · JAPAN
· PRECISELY RAKED GRAVEL INTO
A CHECKERBOARD PATTERN

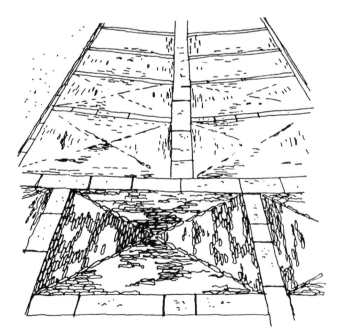

TARRAGONA · SPAIN
· ROUNDED COBBLES FRAMED BY FLAT
LIMESTONE FLAGS

GENERAL PRINCIPLES

PONTE DE LIMA · PORTUGAL
· BRIDGE MOTIF AND EDGING
REPEATED LIKE A SCREEN
PRINT TO GIVE THE SIDEWALK
A DECORATIVE QUALITY

PORTO · PORTUGAL
· CONTRASTING STONE SETTS IN VARIOUS
PATTERNS GIVE THE PAVEMENTS A
DISTINCTIVE CHARACTER

GUIMARÃES · PORTUGAL
· BOLD YET SIMPLE FLORAL
PATTERN EDGED WITH A WIDE
DARK BAND
· VERY STRIKING EFFECT

LEVIS STRAUSS · SAN FRANCISCO
· SENSITIVE TRANSITION BETWEEN
ASPHALT PATH AND TURF USING
GRANITE SETTS

COBBLERS SQUARE · CHICAGO
· COURTYARD PAVING
· INFORMAL BRICK EDGING INFILLED
  WITH IN SITU CONCRETE AND
  SCORED

QUADRANGLE · DALLAS · USA
· STONE GRID ON THE DIAGONAL
· POLISHED GRANITE AT THE
  INTERSECTIONS
· BANDS OF TURF AND PANELS OF
  IN SITU CONCRETE

SURREY DOCKS · LONDON
· COMBINATION OF STONE SETTS
RED PREMIX AND CONCRETE
ROADSTONES
· MATERIALS DEFINE SITTING AREAS
FROM THE FOOTPATH AND CYCLE
ROUTE

NANZENJI · KYOTO · JAPAN
· SQUARE FLAGS SET ON THE
DIAGONAL WITH A NARROW STONE
EDGING AND COBBLE INFILL

SINGAPORE
· FOOTPATH IN SMOOTH CONCRETE
SLABS WITH ROUGH TEXTURED
COBBLES AROUND THE TREE

ATRANI · ITALY
· COMBINATION OF WHITE MARBLE AND
  DEEP PURPLE SETTS LAID IN FANS
· STAR MARKS THE CENTRE OF THE
  PIAZZA

ST MARY'S CATHEDRAL ·
SAN FRANCISCO · USA
· BOLD PAVING DESIGN WITH RED
  BRICK AND TRAVERTINE LIKE AN
  ENTRANCE RUG

LES HALLES · PARIS · FRANCE
· SWIRLING DESIGN OF LIGHT AND
  DARK STONE SETTS

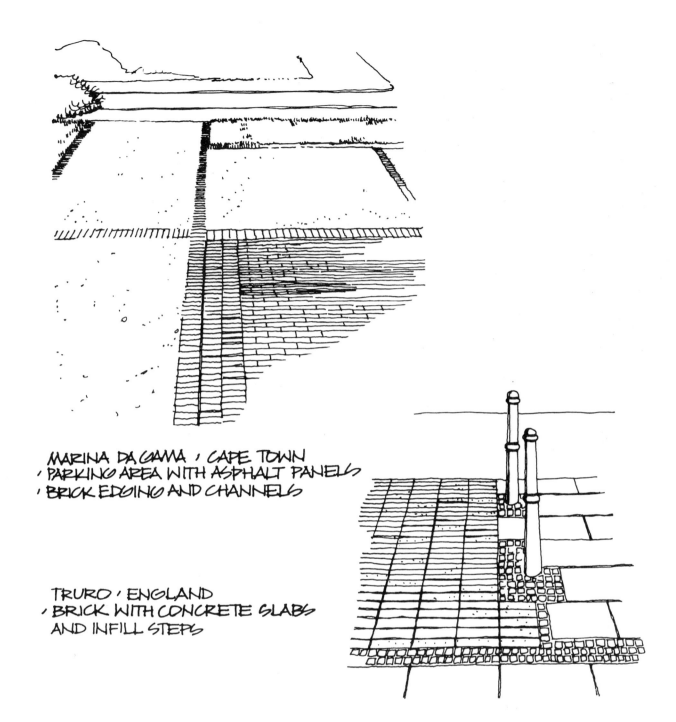

MARINA DA GAMA, CAPE TOWN
, PARKING AREA WITH ASPHALT PANELS
, BRICK EDGING AND CHANNELS

TRURO, ENGLAND
, BRICK WITH CONCRETE SLABS
AND INFILL STEPS

UNIVERSITY OF MEXICO
, BRICK AND STONE SLABS
, EDGING WITH SMALLER
PEBBLES

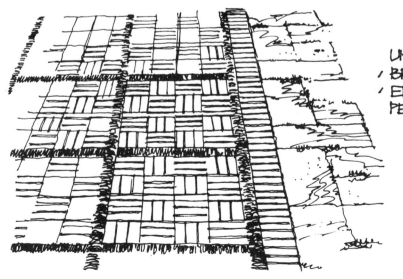

TSUKUBA SCIENCE CITY · JAPAN
· INCREDIBLE ATTENTION TO DETAIL
DISPLAYED BY THE WAY THIS COVER IS NOT
ALLOWED TO INTERRUPT THE INTEGRITY OF
THE PAVING

Kerbs
Channels

Kerbs
Channels

KERBS

SELECTION

The type of kerb should be selected according to:

- Type of barrier required.
- Road class.
- Surrounding paving materials.

ROAD CLASS

Standard barrier kerbs are usually used for safety reasons for road classes 1–3 including, for example, trunk roads, primary distributors, district distributors. For class 4 and 5 roads, namely local distributors and residential access roads, and including parking lots, alternative designs may be considered.

Design aspects include:

- Overall kerb height.
- Angle of kerb line.
- Material and colour.
- Compressive strength.
- Shear strength.

MATERIALS

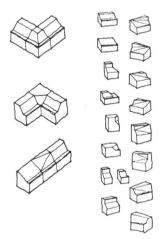

Concrete is the most widely used kerb, offering strength and durability as well as economy. Granite stone kerbs should be retained where possible as part of the city's heritage and also as the most hard wearing kerbing material.

Bricks and cobbles are useful alternatives to concrete kerbs, particularly in residential areas. The interest in 'special' kerbs has resulted in a good response from manufacturers with an increased selection of pre-formed clay and concrete roll-over kerbs. Most products are manufactured with accessories such as dropped kerb setts, tapered units for a variety of radii, external and internal returns.

If standard barrier kerbs are to be used, a finished texture to the concrete may be warranted, with an exposed aggregate or pigment in certain special areas.

DROPPED KERBS

Dropped or ramped kerbs should be provided at all major pedestrian crossings for the convenience of the disabled. Standard transition units between full and dropped kerbs are usually available.

Ramped kerbs can be identified with a change of material. The ramped area should have a surface relief as a warning for blind people.

EDGE RESTRAINTS

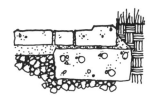

Kerbs help to contain the paving and prevent lateral movement and are therefore an essential part of a flexible paving construction. They are often put down first to form a structural framework and to retain the bedding material on which the paving will be laid.

Flush kerbs may act as a mowing strip adjacent to grassed areas. They should be laid 30 mm below the turf level so as not to obstruct mowing machinery, or 30 mm above the level of planting beds to adequately retain the soil.

DRAINAGE

A combination of kerbs and channels direct the channelling/distribution of stormwater. Profiles which combine the two may prove more economical.

CHANNELS

REQUIREMENTS

Minimum carriageway crossfall on a black-top surface is usually 2%.

A longitudinal channel gradient can be as little as 0.4%.

FLAT SITES

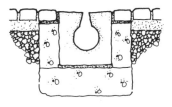

For exceptionally flat sites it may be necessary to use a precast channel system with built-in falls.

STEEP SITES

The principle of distribution rather than concentration may be followed to reduce stormwater buildup at any one point. Textured and/or porous channels may be incorporated to reduce the speed of stormwater and allow absorption of surface water throughout the site. Channels may become an effective irrigation system particularly where trees are planted in paved areas.

DISHED CHANNELS

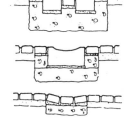

Dished channels can be used to collect stormwater run-off in pedestrian or parking areas and class 5 roads where kerbs are not necessarily required. They usually have a gentle profile with a depth of 50–75 mm and a width ranging from 300–900 mm.

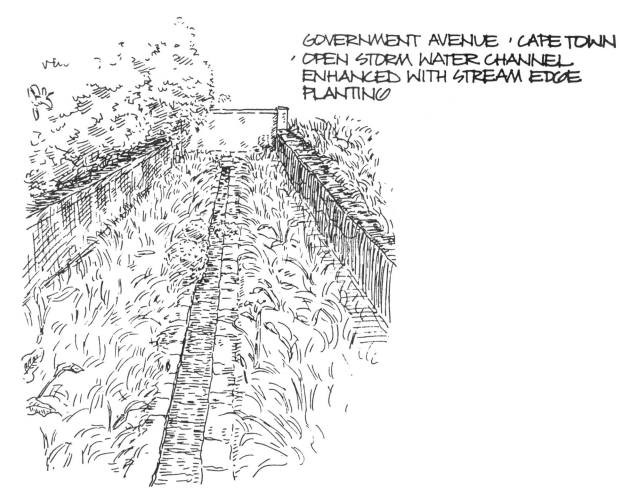

GOVERNMENT AVENUE · CAPE TOWN
· OPEN STORM WATER CHANNEL
ENHANCED WITH STREAM EDGE
PLANTING

MIYAJIMA · JAPAN
· STORMWATER CHANNEL PAVED WITH
COBBLES AND LINED WITH TREES
· THE CHANNEL BECOMES A WATER
FEATURE RATHER THAN A SEWER

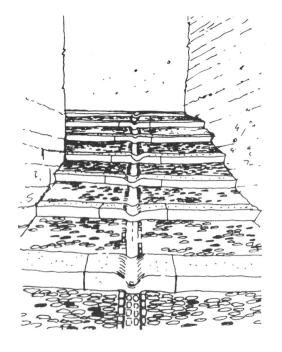

CARCASSONNE · FRANCE
· STONE STEPS WITH CENTRAL
CHANNEL CARVED INTO THE
TREADS

RYOAN - JI · KYOTO · JAPAN
· APPROACH DISHED AND CENTRALLY PAVED
TO DOUBLE AS A CHANNEL FOR RAIN
WATER
· TIMBERS HELP TO DEFLECT WATER AND
PREVENT GULLIES FROM FORMING IN
THE GRAVEL

OXFORD · ENGLAND
· U-SHAPED CHANNEL CONSTRUCTED
OF GRANITE SETTS SEPARATES
GRAVEL AND COBBLED PAVING

COVENT GARDEN · LONDON
· GRANITE SETTS FORM A DISHED
CHANNEL AND DEFINE THE PAVED
ROADWAY

Steps

Steps

USES

Steps can be seen as another dimension of paving, accommodating changes in level, helping to define spaces and even providing outdoor seating.

STEP DIMENSIONS

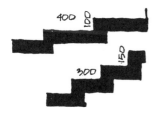

For comfort and safety, outdoor steps are usually a minimum width of 1.5 m and should preferably have at least three risers to a flight. The relationship between tread (T) and riser (R) can be calculated using the formula 2R + T = 600 to 700. The maximum height of an external riser should be 150 mm, but 80 mm to 120 mm is more suitable outdoors.

STEP RHYTHM

A rhythm should be set for a safe descent or ascent by maintaining consistent riser and tread dimensions.

In certain situations, however, where steps do not form part of a through route, the rhythm may be changed to provide for instance access to seating areas where the treads may be lowered and lengthened to respond to the slower moving pedestrian.

STEP PROFILES

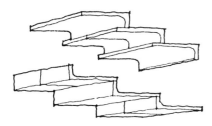

The nose of each tread should be identified were possible in the interest of safety. This can be achieved by:

- A change in bond pattern, material or colour;
- Projecting the nose to create a shadow line.

Bull-noses or rounded noses help to minimise damage to the nose of a tread but identification of the step edge may become less well defined.

RAMPS

Ramps should have a maximum gradient of 1:12 for wheelchairs and prams (1:15 is preferable, and ramps no steeper than 1:20 should be used around hospitals). Surfaces should be non-slip and surface water should be shed across the slope of the ramp.

STEPPED RAMPS

Stepped ramps are useful on long slopes as they enable a steady ascent and can be negotiated by prams and accompanied wheelchairs. Risers should be clearly marked and should not exceed 100 mm. Treads may be as little as 450 mm, but should preferably measure about 1 m for a comfortable stride.

The gradient of a tread should be a maximum of 1:12. For variety, a set of two or three steps can be introduced between ramped sections as long as they are clearly marked.

STEPS & RAMPS

A combination of ramps and steps can be used to break up long flights and provide access for the handicapped. The transition between step and ramp may be detailed with either a projecting or feathered end to the step.

LEVEL CHANGE

A level change of just a few steps within a pedestrian street can be useful as a separating element between stationary and moving pedestrians, or between pedestrians and vehicles. Activities such as outdoor eating, window shopping and seating can occur at the higher level where a sense of security from passing traffic is created, as well as improved viewing.

STEPPED SEATING

Where viewing is an important activity along river frontages, promenades and beachfronts for example, elevated areas can be used to provide seating opportunities. Treads for such areas should be generously designed to function as steps or seats.

SAFETY

Steps, particularly in public areas, should be clearly identified and meet local building regulations such as number of steps in a flight, arrangement and width of landings, and position of balustrades.

LIGHTING

Adequate illumination of a change of level is essential, particularly at the foot and top of a flight.

KATSURA PALACE · KYOTO · JAPAN
· QUITE SERENE ATTENTION TO
  FORM AND TEXTURE

TOSHODAIJI · NARA · JAPAN
· STONE STEPS CONNECTING GRAVEL PATH
  WITH RAISED TIMBER DECK
· STEPS ALSO BRIDGE DRAINAGE CHANNEL

KATSURA PALACE · KYOTO · JAPAN
· AN ORIGINAL STEPPED RAMP
· STEPPING STONES EMERGE FROM
  THE COBBLED PAVING IN A
  RANDOM BUT WELL PROPORTIONED
  PATTERN

MILAN / ITALY
· SEATING STEPS CLAD IN MARBLE
· GENEROUS TREADS TO ALLOW
  FOR FEET · BUMS AND ACCESS
  IN BETWEEN

TSUKUBA / JAPAN
· STEPS CUT INTO SEATING TREADS
· FLAMED GRANITE TREADS
· ROUGH HEWN RISERS

SISSINGHURST · KENT · ENGLAND
· BRICK STEPS WITH A LOW RISER
AND WIDE TREAD
· STEPS AND WALL CONSTRUCTION
COORDINATED

WASHINGTON D.C. · USA
· STEPS AND PLANTER WALLS FORM
PART OF THE SAME STONE
CONSTRUCTION

GENERAL PRINCIPLES

RYOAN -JI · KYOTO · JAPAN
· A BEAUTIFUL COMPOSITION OF STEPS ·
PLANTING · PAVING AND FENCING
· AN EASY TREAD / RISER PROPORTION

J. F. KENNEDY LIBRARY · BOSTON
· SCULPTURAL FORMS DISTINGUISH
  THIS BUILDING
· STEPS RADIATING IN A SWEEPING
  GEOMETRY

TSUKUBA · JAPAN
· GRANITE IMPERFECTION EXPLOITED
  TO CREATE A STUNNING TRANSITION
  OF MATERIALS WHILE CHANGING
  LEVEL

GENERAL PRINCIPLES

Tree Surrounds
Tree Guards

Tree Surrounds
Tree Guards

TREE SURROUNDS

GRIDS

Tree grids can be used to maintain paving continuity and to protect and ventilate root systems. They also allow irrigation by surface water run off.

DESIGN THEME

Although materials may vary with location, the basic tree grid size and shape might follow a design theme, to enhance the paving continuity and pattern in one specific area.

TREE GROWTH

The inner sections of the tree grid should be removable to allow for tree growth, or made suitably generous at the outset.

PROTECTION AND SEATING

Trees in parking areas or other trafficked zones, can be protected by a rubbing kerb of brick or setts.

The design of the surround may be set at seat height, especially in pedestrian areas. The tree is thereby protected while offering shaded integral seating.

MINIMUM DIMENSIONS

Tree surrounds should be a minimum of 1 m square to allow sufficient aeration of the soil, but this will depend on the ultimate size of the tree and related root system.

MATERIALS

Tree grids should reflect their location through choice of material and detail. The local architectural character, or existing historic street furniture, may influence selection.

- *Cast iron*: a high grade ductile (non-breakable) cast iron or grey iron should be specified. This traditional material is durable and can be cast into highly decorative patterns more readily than any other material. The material suits almost every type of environment, and is particularly appropriate in historic areas.

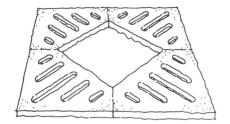

- *Concrete*: less intricate patterning is possible with precast concrete but the material may be used to match the surrounding paving pattern, and maintain material continuity. A smooth, dimpled or exposed aggregate finish can be specified. Some reinforcing mesh is usually required.

- *Individual paving units*: concrete, brick or cobbles, may be set into a coarse sand bedding with sand joints. The advantages are the flexibility of being able to remove individual units gradually as the tree grows. The disadvantages are that unfixed units may be susceptible to vandalism and that the initial porous nature of the sand joints may in time become blocked with dirt and form an impervious surface or encourage growth of weeds and moss.

STAKING

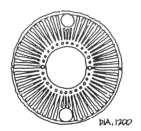

If tree stakes are required the grid should be selected to allow for such staking to be installed through the grid. Grids may be designed to be set in secured frames from which trees can be steadied by wire stays.

SUB-FRAMES

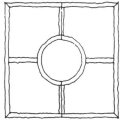

A frame to receive the grid is preferable to prevent the differential settlement of individual sections of a grid. The frames are fixed under adjoining paving and act as a paving restraint, or can be positioned on their own foundation.

CONSTRUCTION SEQUENCE

All surrounds and fittings should be fabricated in two or more pieces so that these may be fitted after tree planting, particularly where large root balls are specified.

SPARE PARTS

It is wise to include the provision of replacement parts when ordering. Also to make sure that patterns are retained.

INTEGRAL FITTINGS

A number of accessories can be incorporated or attached to a tree grid system such as:

- *Lighting*: up-lighting from pavement level in certain controlled environments can create special floodlit effects. Appropriate vandal-proof flush fittings are available and can be designed into porthole patterns.

- *Irrigation*: automatic irrigation or a perforated pipe wrapped around the root ball will encourage downward root growth. Such equipment or pipe-ends should be incorporated into the grid and secured with a flush locking plate.

- *Tree guard*: tree guards and grids should be coordinated where they occur together, in terms of fixing and detail.

TREE GUARDS

FUNCTION

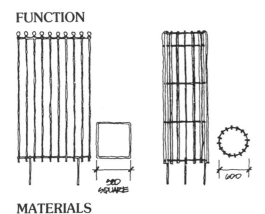

Tree guards give newly planted trees protection in intensively used pedestrian areas. These areas include car parks, supermarkets, or in narrow pavements. Tree guards wrap round the tree and are bolted or staked through the grid to a below-ground fixing. Alternatively, low rails may be incorporated and fixed in a similar manner.

Guards or railings can also double as staking for trees.

MATERIALS

Mild steel is particularly suitable in a city context incorporating appropriate anti-corrosive protection.

IDENTITY

Tree guards and railings can be designed within the same theme, using a standard language throughout the city, or with variation in specific locations.

HEIGHT

Tree guards should stand between 1.3 and 1.6 m high to give adequate protection, and should not interfere with the branching of the tree. Where guards have spiked ends, these should point outwards to prevent damage to the tree.

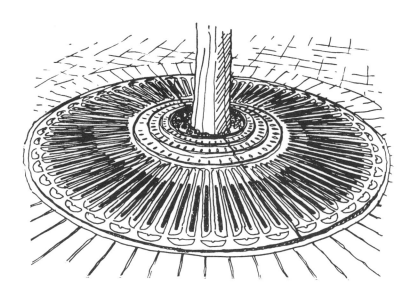

MUSEUM OF MODERN ART · WASHINGTON D.C.
· CAST IRON TREE GRID
· UNUSUALLY FINE DETAIL CREATED BY
RECESSED AND PERFORATED PATTERNS

TOKYO · JAPAN
· NEAT FLUSH CIRCULAR CAST IRON
GRID IN THREE SECTIONS

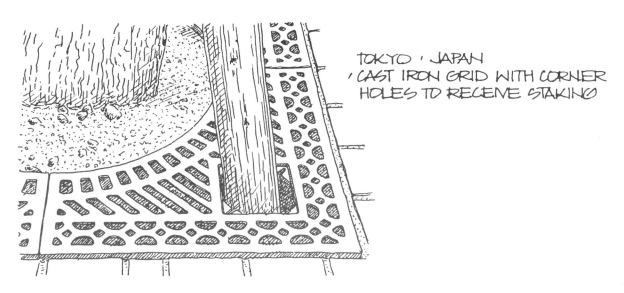

TOKYO · JAPAN
· CAST IRON GRID WITH CORNER
HOLES TO RECEIVE STAKING

EMBARCADERO 2 · SAN FRANCISCO
· TREE SURROUNDS PROTECT TREES AND ALSO
PROVIDE SEATING AT THE ENTRANCE TO THE
PARK

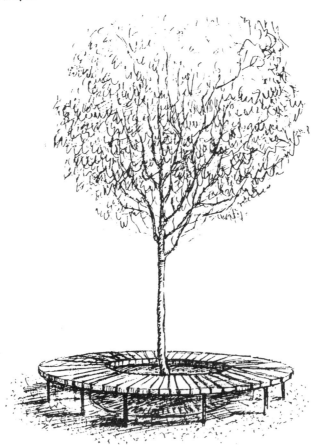

ATLANTA · GEORGIA · USA
· TIMBER SLATTED TREE SURROUND
AT SEAT HEIGHT

OCEAN PARK · HONG KONG
· TREE SURROUND DETAILED
  WITH FLAT SECTIONS
· INCONSPICUOUS FIXING AND
  ROBUST EDGE PROTECTION

SAN FRANCISCO · CALIFORNIA · USA
· SIMPLE TREE GUARDS BOLTED TO
  TREE GRID

NICOLLET MALL · MINNEAPOLIS · USA
· TREE SURROUNDS EXTEND TO FORM
  LIGHTING SUPPORTS
· SOLID BASE FOR TREE GUARD FIXING

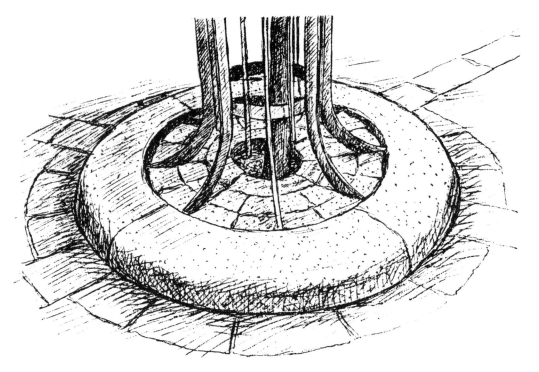

OCEAN PARK · HONG KONG
· LOOSE LAID GRANITE SETTS RECEIVE
  TREE SURROUND
· CIRCULAR STONE KERBING FOR PROTECTION

HIMEJI · JAPAN
· SERIES OF NARROW BARS FORMS GRID
· EDGING OF GRANITE SETTS CONTRAST
  WITH SMOOTH BLACK TILE PAVING

WASHINGTON D.C · U.S.A
· GRANITE SETTS OPEN JOINTED
  AND RESTRAINED BY A CAST
  IRON COLLAR

TOKYO · JAPAN
· TREES PLANTED ALTERNATELY IN
GRASS VERGE AND PAVING
· SMALL GRID DESIGNED TO TAKE
STAKING

DURBAN · RSA
· CONCRETE TREE GRID IN FOUR
SECTIONS WITH SURFACE TEXTURE
TO MATCH SURROUNDING SLABS

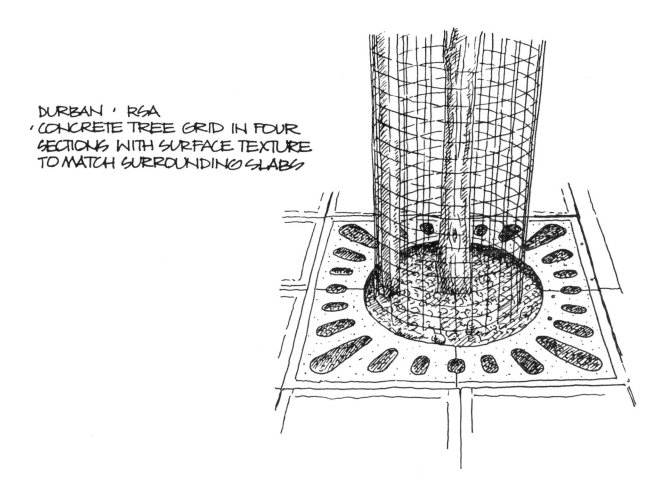

MINNEAPOLIS · MINNESOTA · USA
· TUBULAR TREE SURROUNDS TO CREATE
  A SEAT AND BACKREST
· A CLEAN CONTEMPORARY FEEL

STATE STREET MALL · CHICAGO
· EXPOSED AGGREGATE CIRCULAR
  SEATING CONTAINS SHRUB AND
  TREE PLANTING

Seating
Amphitheatres

Seating
Amphitheatres

SELECTION

Seating is normally selected for short or long term use. Long term seating has greater comfort requirements, such as a more moulded shape with back and arm rests for park and mall seating. Short term seating can be simpler and more versatile, such as benches integrated with planters and walls, or perch seating at bus stops.

SITING

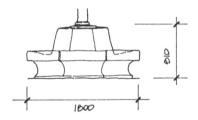

Seating may be organised in a variety of ways:

- Inward looking for conversation.
- Outward looking, back to back with a view.
- Seating in the hub of activity, in malls and plazas.
- Individual seats for bus stops, cafes.
- Modular seating which, in small units, can take a curvalinear form, useful for wrapping around and between trees.
- Secluded seating integrated with planting to create a place of quiet privacy.

Where possible, seating should be located with protection from the elements, particularly the wind. There should be a logic to the arrangement to avoid 'floating' benches which tend simply to clutter or obstruct pedestrian areas.

CRITERIA

Factors to consider when selecting seating designs are:

- Comfort,
- Stability,
- Heat absorbtion,
- Water run off efficiency,
- Low maintenance,
- Robustness against vandalism.

MATERIALS

Certain materials form more inviting surfaces to sit on. Timber is a particularly warm material. Metals and stone, although practical and comfortable, are cold surfaces to sit on for any length of time.

- *Timber* looks appropriate in both historic and contemporary contexts. The timber should, of course, be dressed all round, planed, sanded and splinter free. Hardwoods are particularly durable, but should only be carefully specified from an approved renewable source.

- *Perforated metal sheeting*, wire mesh or expanded metal are hard wearing materials which are particularly suitable in urban environments.

- *Cast metals* allow a quality of detailing unobtainable in other materials, but are rarely used for the actual seat material.

The support system may be either tubular metal, cast iron or aluminium, concrete, stone or timber.

MAINTENANCE OF MATERIALS

Low maintenance materials are preferable. Any metal should be treated appropriately against corrosion, including assembly fixings. Metals can be protected with hard wearing finishes such as a factory powder coating, applied electro-statically. Stainless steel and marine quality aluminium should be considered in coastal areas or where intensive use would damage any finish. Supermarkets should be considered in this category. Timbers should be treated against rot and concretes may be sealed.

Materials that do not deteriorate under the extremities of heat and cold, or wet and dry conditions, should be selected.

ANTI-VANDALISM

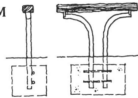

Benches in areas of possible vandalism should incorporate holding-down bolts, or sub-surface built in anchorage.

PROPORTIONS

Seating may be of many different proportions, but fundamental body characteristics only vary slightly. Anthropometric data should be borne in mind when designing coordinated street furniture. For example, a wall has the possibility of being a seat if built at the right height and with a continuous comfortable coping.

There are certain critical dimensions for an average person:

- *Seat height*: men 440 mm, women 440 mm.
- *Seat depth*: men 480 mm, women 420 mm.
- *Average posterior height*: 720 mm, therefore perch seating may range between 600–650 mm high.
- *Width at hips*: men 370 mm, women 400 mm.

For comfort a lower, deeper seat is preferable, with a height of 395–430 mm and depth of 490–635 mm. Also the more profiled the seat, the more comfortable it is, particularly with the back rest and seat angled gently.

There are many subtleties to seat arrangement design. Between strangers a certain amount of space is usually important for privacy. On a 1.8 m bench, for instance, it is rare to find more than two people, although from the authropometric data four people can fit on it.

Usual bench lengths are 1.2 m, 1.8 m, and 2.4 m. If benches are long enough to lie on, vagrants will use them. Intermediate arm rests can be incorporated to prevent this.

TABLE SEATS

In areas of open circulation, benches with backs and armrests may be too directional. A low wide bench, almost square, is useful in this situation where a newspaper may be laid out and read, or where people may sit on any of the four sides choosing their aspect.

MODULAR SEATING

Systems of modular seating allow flexibility in length and arrangement. Long continuous benches may be appropriate at nodal points where people are known to congregate, or for particular viewing purposes.

FIXING

On level sites, benches may be bolted to paving. On sloping sites, ground fixing may be preferable to enable the bench to be set level and to maintain a clear uncluttered appearance. All fixings should be countersunk and plugged.

WALL SEATS

Walls can be designed with recesses to receive seating which can be on ledges, bracketed or remain free-standing. Individual seats can be mounted on to low retaining walls.

AMPHITHEATRES

MATERIALS

Amphitheatres may be designed as an area of terraced grass or stepped concrete or stone. Materials should be selected appropriate to location: grassed terraces for informal parkland seating; hard paved amphitheatres for seating formal or large scale gatherings such as concerts.

Seating material can either be incorporated into the structure itself or a bolted-on surface material such as timber or framed perforated metal sheeting can be used.

DIMENSIONS

The treads of the steps should be generous enough to allow access behind seated people, for example 900 mm wide.

OCEAN PARK, HONG KONG
· WATER EDGE AMPHITHEATRE FORMS
A CRISP MARGIN TO THE LAKE

U. C. SANTA CRUZ, CALIFORNIA, USA
· AMPHITHEATRE SCULPTED OUT OF
A QUARRY
· TIMBER SEATING WITH GRAVEL IN
BETWEEN FOR CIRCULATION

TOKYO , JAPAN
· PUBLIC SEATING FOR
INDIVIDUAL RECLINING

PIONEER SQUARE · SEATTLE
· TIMBER SLATTED BENCHES WITH GENEROUS
CIRCULAR ARM RESTS AS A FEATURE

TSUKUBA · JAPAN
· TIMBER SLATTED BENCH
· SQUARE SECTION FRAME WITH HALF
ROUND TIMBERS FOR ARM REST
COMFORT

MIT · BOSTON · USA
· SQUARE SECTION STEEL SUPPORT
· PERFORATED TIMBER BACK AND
SEAT IN NATURAL FINISH

SURREY DOCKS · LONDON
· HIGH BACK INDIVIDUAL SEATS
· CONTOURED FOR COMFORT
· LIGHT WEIGHT STEEL FRAME · PAINTED

CHURCH STREET · CAPE TOWN
· REPRODUCTION 'REGENCY'
· FLAT IRON SECTIONS

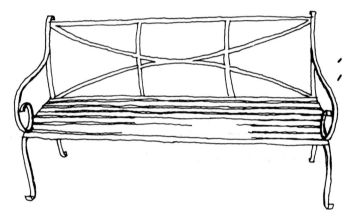

COBBLERS SQUARE · CHICAGO · USA
· ELEGANT CURVEY BENCH OF FLAT SECTION
STEEL SUPPORTED TOP AND BOTTOM ONLY

GENERAL PRINCIPLES

TOKYO / JAPAN
・CAST IRON INDIVIDUAL SEATS
・SUPPORTED ON A CONTINUOUS BACK BAR
・COMFORTABLE AND ELEGANT

DALLAS · TEXAS · USA
· CONTRASTS OF MATERIALS AND WEIGHTS
· HEAVY STONE PROFILED BENCH ENDS
· CLOSELY SPACED AND CURVED STEEL BARS
· MATCHING BOLLARD

EMBARCADERO · SAN FRANCISCO
· CHUNKY TIMBER DOUBLE SIDED BENCH
  WITH CONCRETE ENDS
· STURDY WATERFRONT DESIGN

GENERAL PRINCIPLES

SEGESTA , SICILY
, STONE BENCH IN THE TEMPLE GROUNDS
, APPROPRIATE DESIGN FOR ITS SETTING
IN TERMS OF PROPORTION AND DETAIL

TOKYO , JAPAN
, BIG LUMP OF GRANITE POLISHED ON
ITS TOP SURFACE TO FORM A STONE
BENCH

QUINCY MARKET, BOSTON
, LARGE CIRCULAR SEAT /
TABLE FOR SPREADING OUT
A NEWSPAPER AND LUNCH

BOSTON , USA
, PRECAST CONCRETE STEP / SEAT
, FOR SHORT TERM 'PERCH' SEATING

BOSTON , USA
, SIMPLE CONCRETE FORMS COORDINATE
LIGHTING AND SEATING

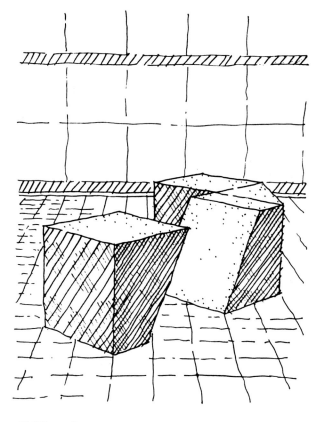

MIT / BOSTON / USA
· SCULPTURAL FORMS IN STONE AS SEATS
· SURROUNDING CONTEMPORARY CLEAN
  LINED ARCHITECTURE

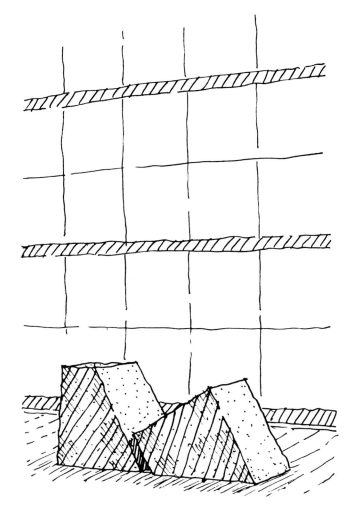

EMBARCADERO · SAN FRANCISCO · USA
· SUNNY RECLINING SEATING
· IN SITU CONCRETE CONSTRUCTION

U.C. SANTA CRUZ · CALIFORNIA · USA
· AMPHITHEATRE SEATING
· TIMBER BENCHING IN PAIRS
· CONFIGURATION DESIGNED LIKE
  CONTOURS TO BLEND INTO WOODLAND
  SETTING

LORING GREENWAY · MINNEAPOLIS · USA
· ALMOST SQUARE TIMBER TABLE / SEATS
· LARGE TIMBER SECTIONS 'SCOOPED OUT'
  TO FORM DOUBLE SIDED SEAT

U.C. SANTA CRUZ , CALIFORNIA
, CHUNKY TIMBER BENCH
, SEAT PLANKS OVERSAILING MAIN
SUPPORT

EXPO' 86 , VANCOUVER , CANADA
, WATERSIDE BENCH
, LOW AND WIDE DIMENSIONS
, LARGE TIMBER SECTIONS BOLTED TOGETHER
AND SUPPORTED ON A STEEL 'I' SECTION

TOKYO , JAPAN
, INDIVIDUAL TIMBER SLATTED SEATS
, STEEL DIVIDER ARMRESTS

VANCOUVER EXPO' 86 , CANADA
, STEEL TRUSS SUPPORT SYSTEM
, CONCRETE ENDS WITH LOGO PROTECTS
  THE STRUCTURE AND GIVES IT STABILITY

Planters

Planters

USES

Plant containers can be used where trees and shrubs cannot be planted directly into the ground. They can be used to form barriers, provide visual screening or soften high walls.

SITING

Solitary planters, unrelated to the surrounding streetscape should be avoided. Grouped containers have greater impact and can form secluded spaces for seating.

COORDINATION

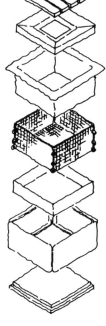

Containers should form an integral part of the streetscape and can be used in conjunction with litter bins, seating, steps and retaining walls.

HANGING BASKETS

Baskets with plants can be hung from light poles but should be confined to special areas and locations where adequate maintenance can be assured.

Baskets may not be a permanent feature and hooks could be provided so that they can be hung for special occasions, or seasonally.

Irrigation for baskets should be considered and either catered for with regular manual maintenance, or by incorporating a water reservoir, or through an automatic irrigation system.

ADAPTABILITY

Free-standing planters are adaptable and allow for stacking and grouping. Stacking provides extra soil depth for tree planting.

TEMPORARY PLANTERS

Short-term containers should be easily transportable. The maximum volume of soil that two men can carry is approximately $600 \times 600 \times 300$ mm or about $0.1 \, m^3$ depending on soil saturation. These are often used for temporary pedestrianisation, and as traffic barriers, or in association with cafes and shops.

GENERAL PRINCIPLES

CAPACITY

Large containers are preferable to minimise the danger of soil dehydration. Large planters can also prove more useful in terms of the range of plant material that can be considered. One cubic metre soil capacity should be provided as a minimum, and preferably with a depth of not less than 350–400 mm.

LONG-TERM PLANTERS

Long-term containers are normally larger and need to be position by fork lift truck, or built *in situ*. These planters may be partly or fully recessed into the ground.

PERMANENT PLANTERS

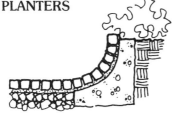

In situ planters can be designed as an extension of the paving using bricks, setts, or *in situ* concrete, although reinforced concrete is recommended where damage may be caused by tree roots.

SERVICES PROTECTION

Bottomless concrete rings can be used to protect services from tree roots although root bars may be more satisfactory. These need only be placed between the tree and the service duct, allowing full root development in all other directions.

PAVEMENT FALLS

The advantage of *in situ* planters is that any fall occurring in the surrounding paving can be accommodated in the design. Free standing planters can cater for falls by some mechanical device incorporated into the design which allows adjustment.

PLANT MATERIAL

Plant materials need to be selected carefully, to display contrasting foliage textures, strong sculptural forms or colours. Bold repetitive groupings of plant types are recommended.

If plants need to be replaced periodically, galvanised wire baskets could be installed, (say four to six per planter) for easy replacement by hand or machine.

CONTAINER FINISHES

Planters should be maintenance-free on a long term basis and resistant to vandalism. They should be robust to survive mechanical handling and positioning, and both scratch and dent proof. The material selected should not be a good conductor of heat as this will increase the chance of soil dehydration.

Finishes should be resistant to atmospheric pollution, and in keeping with surrounding architectural detailing, particularly in conservation areas.

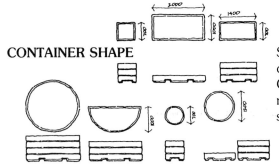

CONTAINER SHAPE

Sharp corners and edges should be avoided in the design of containers. Acute angles are difficult to plant successfully. Circular shapes are overall the most practical although they may not be appropriate architecturally, and do require more space than a square planter of similar capacity.

DRAINAGE

A gravel bed with filter cloth and weepholes should be provided to facilitate drainage.

IRRIGATION

A water reservoir may be incorporated at the base of the container by means of an absorbent mat, or an absorbent inert material such as an agricultural polymer, or system of actual water reservoirs connected to a device which monitors the water level. Preferably, where the budget allows, an automatic irrigation system should be installed to ensure rapid establishment and continuing growth.

TREE STABILITY

Generally sub-surface guying is preferable to staking. It is inconspicuous and therefore less prone to vandalism. Anchor points should be incorporated into planter design. Staking would require a minimum depth of 900 mm to be effective.

CLERKENWELL GREEN · LONDON
· OLD CATTLE TROUGH CONVERTED TO A
PLANTER FOR BULBS AND ANNUALS

RORSCHACH · SWITZERLAND
· CAST ALUMINIUM STREET LAMP
· METAL SUPPORT STRUCTURE
· CONCRETE PEDESTAL
· PROVISION FOR A CREEPER INCORPORATED

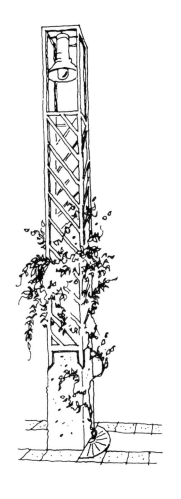

CONSTITUTION PLAZA ' HARTFORD '
CONNECTICUT ' USA
' ROOF TERRACE PLANTING
ACHIEVED BY MOUNDING WITH
LOW CONCRETE RETAINING WALLS
AT SEAT HEIGHT

FISHERMAN'S WHARF '
SAN FRANCISCO ' USA
' TIMBER PLANTER SURROUNDS
CONSTRUCTED TO PROVIDE LOW '
WIDE SEATING
' WELL DESIGNED AND DETAILED

GENERAL PRINCIPLES

SAN FRANCISCO / USA
· PRECAST CONCRETE PLANTERS WITH GRID
PATTERN EMPHASISING MODULAR CONCEPT

EMBARCADERO · SAN FRANCISCO
· LOW DISHED CAST METAL
· UNIFORM PLANT SELECTION
· PLANTERS GROUPED

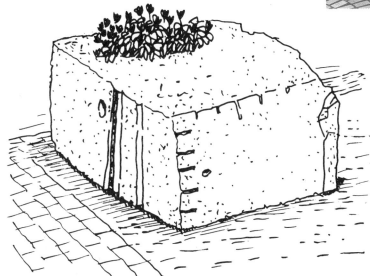

EMBARCADERO / SAN FRANCISCO
· ROUGH HEWN LUMP OF STONE WITH A
HOLE CARVED OUT FOR PLANTING ANNUALS

FISHERMAN'S WHARF , SAN FRANCISCO
, STURDY TIMBER PLANTER
, CONSPICUOUS BOLT FIXINGS
, TIMBER IN NATURAL FINISH

MITCHELL'S PLAIN , CAPE TOWN , RSA
, TIMBER PLANTERS
, INTEGRAL STAKING FOR TREES
, GROUPED FOR PLANTING IMPACT

INSTITUTE OF JAPANESE ARCHITECTS ,
TOKYO , JAPAN
, TIMBER PLANTER WITH METAL STRAPS

SECESSION BUILDING · VIENNA · AUSTRIA
· BEAUTIFULLY RESTORED MOSAICED PLANTER
· BOWL STABILISED WITH CAST IRON TORTOISES

ROBIE HOUSE · CHICAGO · USA
· WIDE SHALLOW PLANTER
· ELEGANT LINES TO MATCH THE
  HOUSE ARCHITECTURE

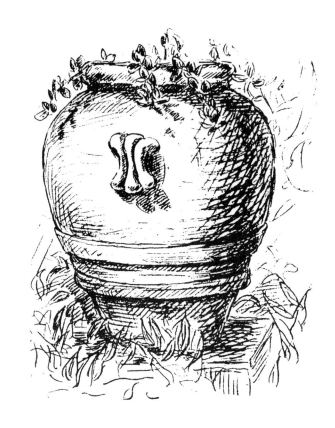

SISSINGHURST · KENT · ENGLAND
· LARGE TERRACOTTA POT

Litter Bins

Litter Bins

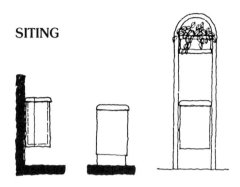

SITING

Bins should be visible and convenient, but not obtrusive.

Bins do not necessarily require separate poles but could be fixed to lamp-posts, bus stops, street signage, or may be wall-mounted or free-standing.

In linear situations along a high street, bins could be sited at 30 m intervals, but this may be increased outside particular fast food outlets, cinemas, sweetshops, or decreased outside certain civic buildings for security reasons.

CAPACITY

The minimum capacity for a litter bin in the city centre should be 50 litres. In large areas or along busy sidewalks, pedestal bins with a capacity of 50 to 100 litres may be more appropriate.

MAINTENANCE

Capacity and maintenance are directly related. Bins become pointless unless regularly cleared. Bin location and anticipated frequency of emptying will determine the litter bin capacity.

COORDINATION

The material and colour should be coordinated with other street furniture elements. Simple rectangular or circular shapes are preferable.

CRITERIA

Factors that need to be considered in bin design are:

- Robustness against vandalism and wear.
- Low maintenance materials.
- Ease of emptying and cleaning.
- Theftproof.
- Fireproof to a specific fire retardancy factor.
- Concealment of contents.
- Mounting and fixing components.

MATERIALS

Materials should combine strength with durability:

- *Glass reinforced polyster*: manufactured from fire retarded resins have a 'wipe clean' surface required in certain controlled environments.
- *Cast metals*: may incorporate a high level of detail, including site specific graphics or logos. They are strong and allow for more elegant designs without loss of robustness.
- *Concrete*: requires little maintenance, but the thickness' of the material means that only simple forms may be achieved. Exposed aggregate finishes give a textured, economic and long-lasting effect.
- *Timber*: should be considered only with a steel bin lining. It is a relatively unobtrusive material and suits both formal and informal environments.

Liners may be fabricated of galvanized steel, plastic-coated wire mesh or polyethelene.

LIDS

Where possible litter should be concealed. Lids help to reduce smell and minimise insect attraction, as well as prevent litter from being blown about by the wind.

Lids may be removable, on a chain, or fixed with a hinge door on the proven British 'pillar box' principle. All opening devices should be quick and simple to operate.

DRAINAGE

Drainage holes should be provided for periodic flushing out and to allow rainwater to disperse.

SECURITY

Where security is an important factor, the bin contents should be visible. Pedestal bins for instance with an open top are particularly suitable. It may be that bins are not located at all in high security areas. Various techniques have been developed to reduce the shrapnel effect of bins in bomb blast situations.

ADVERTISING AND SPONSORSHIP

Sponsorship of bins may be combined with advertising to promote 'keep clean' campaigns, particularly in busy city centres.

LES HALLES · PARIS · FRANCE
· ELEGANT TALL THIN LITTER BIN
WITH TOP FLARED OPEN

HIMEJI / JAPAN
· SLATTED TIMBER LITTER BIN
· PERFORATED STEEL LINER
· BIN CONTENTS PARTIALLY CONCEALED
  FROM VIEW WITH HINGED LID

MINNEAPOLIS / USA
· TIMBER CLAD BIN
· STAINLESS STEEL LID WITH
  BENT STEEL HANDLE AND
  OPENING COVER

FISHERMAN'S WHARF / SAN FRANCISCO
· TIMBER LITTER BIN
· CONSPICUOUS ARCHITECTURAL GRAPHICS

LITTER BINS

VANCOUVER · CANADA
· DECORATIVE STEEL 'CAGE' CONTAINING
A STAINLESS STEEL BIN LINER

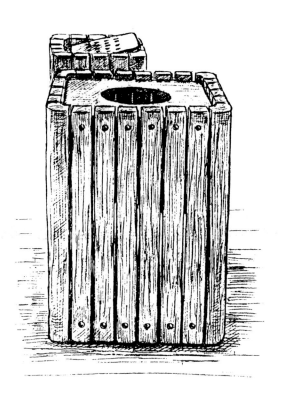

TOKYO · JAPAN
· TIMBER LITTER AND CIGARETTE BINS
· STEEL TOP PLATE PERFORATED

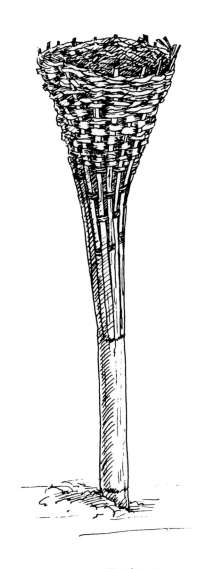

CHAING MAI · THAILAND
· INGENIOUS LITTER BIN MADE
FROM A SINGLE BAMBOO CANE
SPLIT AND WOVEN TO FORM
A CONTAINER

TOBACCO DOCKS, LONDON
, LITTER BIN COMBINED WITH PLANTER
, COLOURS: GUN METAL WITH
  PILLAR BOX RED LATTICE OF FLAT
  SECTION STEEL
, STENCIL CUT OUT LETTERING

Bollards

Bollards

FUNCTIONAL USE

Bollards form a useful barrier for vehicles and can be used as a substitute for kerbs or in combination with them. Bollards should however be carefully located to avoid unnecessary street clutter and obstruction.

Low bollards can be used for seating or to accommodate low level lighting in pedestrian and parking areas.

HISTORIC AREAS

Cast-iron Victorian bollards had a particularly decorative quality, and today many reproductions are available. Care should be taken that contemporary designs blend well in conservation areas.

MATERIALS

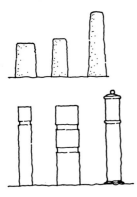

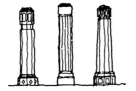

Suitable materials with good durability characteristics are:

- *Precast concrete*: the amount and type of detailing is restricted by the nature of the material, but logos and simple patterns can successfully be included in the moulding process. An exposed aggregate finish could match adjacent paving materials, and is a relatively maintenance-free option. Concrete is also relatively inexpensive if a standard mould is used.

- *Steel*: this is a common substitute for cast iron, although not as durable. Steel relies on appropriate preparation, such as galvanizing, prior to painting, and the application of a protective coating is of particular importance to ensure resistance to corrosion. Decoration is usually achieved by welding on bars and plates.

- *Cast iron*: only spheroidal graphite (ductile/non-breakable cast iron) should be used. This has greater tensile strength than grey iron. The material can be cut and welded as with steel, and has a high corrosive resistance.

- *Aluminium*: a lightweight material which is not recommended for heavily trafficked areas. A high silicon type such as LM6 is preferable. Many moulded aluminium forms that are available, are replicas of earlier cast-iron designs.

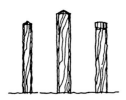

- *Timber*: requires little maintenance and weathers naturally. Hardwoods should be specified carefully from a known approved and renewable source. Wood can be sculpted or routed out to create additional decorative features. The section below ground level is often treated with bitumen to give protection from rot.

SPACING

The spacing between bollards should be approximately 1.5 m where a barrier for vehicular access is required, but may be wider if used in conjunction with a chain or rail.

REMOVABLE BOLLARDS

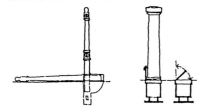

Where emergency or service access is required, removable bollards should be used. The bollard either slots into a sleeve in the ground, or metal versions may be hinged and/or locked.

HEIGHT

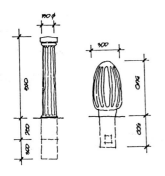

In parking areas where cars might reverse against a bollard, they should be high enough to be seen from a driving position, which implies a suitable height ranging between 0.9 m and 1.2 m high.

In pedestrian areas they may be installed at a much lower level, the exact height is dependent on the proportions and design of the bollard. There will always be some additional length for below-ground fixing. Where there is a possibility of impact from vehicles, this below-ground dimension should be increased for additional stability.

VISIBILITY

A recess for a reflective band can be incorporated into the design for extra visibility at night.

VISIBLE KERB REINFORCEMENT

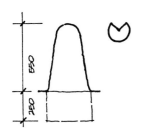

The vertical nature of a bollard means that it is a useful visible element to identify pedestrian cross-overs, pinch points in the road, and generally where kerb reinforcement is required, or as protection of architectural elements such as the corners of buildings.

FISHERMAN'S WHARF : SAN FRANCISCO
· OLD TELEGRAPH POLES CUT WITH A
  CHAMFERED TOP TO FORM BOLLARDS
· BOLLARDS CONNECTED WITH A STURDY
  CHAIN

MILAN · ITALY
· BUSH HAMMERED STONE BOLLARDS
· CONNECTING CHAIN TOP FIXED WITH
  ROBUST BUT ELEGANT DETAILING

COVENT GARDEN · LONDON · UK
· SQUARE SECTION TIMBER BOLLARDS
· MATERIAL SELECTION SUITS MARKET
  ATMOSPHERE EVEN IN AN URBAN
  CONTEXT

MOULINS · FRANCE
· BOLLARDS WITH 'TYING UP' RAIL FOR
  MARKET DAY
· TRIO OF BOLLARDS SPACED BETWEEN
  TREES IN ALIGNMENT

BERCY · PARIS · FRANCE
· ROAD WIDTH RESTRICTION WITH
  LOW PRECAST CONCRETE BOLLARDS
· NO KERBING REQUIRED

HIMEJI , JAPAN
, ROUGH HEWN GRANITE BOLLARDS
CLOSELY SPACED WITH LIGHT WEIGHT
STAINLESS STEEL CHAINS

MILAN , ITALY
, GRANITE BOLLARDS WITH CHAIN
, UNUSUAL CHAIN FIXING

GENERAL PRINCIPLES

PARIS / FRANCE
/ CONCRETE FULL HEIGHT AND
SHORT BOLLARD VERSION

COPLEY SQUARE / BOSTON USA
/ CONCRETE BOLLARDS
/ ARTICULATION WITH RECESSES

LEVIS STRAUSS / EMBARCADERO / SAN FRANCISCO
/ BUSH HAMMERED GRANITE BOLLARDS
/ LOW AND GENEROUS DIAMETER WITH
CHAIN FIXING

SCIENCE MUSEUM · HAMAMATSU · JAPAN
· CIRCULAR 'PLANETARY' BOLLARDS
· CONCRETE WITH A RECESS FOR A
REFLECTIVE BAND

MUSEUM OF MODERN ART
WASHINGTON D.C. · USA
· LOW GRANITE BOLLARDS SET
CLOSELY TOGETHER WITH
MATCHING GRANITE SETT PAVING

HOUT BAY · CAPE TOWN · RSA
· HARBOUR SIDE BOLLARD
· HEAVY BASE PLATE DETAIL AND
ARMS TO SECURE ROPES

KYOTO , JAPAN
' ORNATELY CARVED STONE BOLLARDS
' EACH ONE DIFFERENT
' MATCHING STONE KERB AND SLABS

GOVERNMENT AVENUE , CAPE TOWN
, ORIGINAL CAST IRON BOLLARD

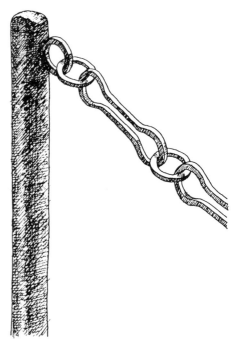

TURIN , ITALY
, BOLLARD WITH BEAUTIFULLY
ENGINEERED HEAVY CHAIN

VIENNA , AUSTRIA
, SHORT CAST IRON BOLLARDS
, POSITIONED ALONG A KERB
TURNING IN TOWARDS THE PAVEMENT
, BENT DETAIL FOR SOME MYSTERIOUS
FUNCTION OR AS A PRACTICAL JOKE!

GENERAL PRINCIPLES

Balustrades
Railings
Fencing

Balustrades
Railings
Fencing

BALUSTRADES

FUNCTION

Balustrades tend to be used as a supportive or safety element at changes of level.

HEIGHT

Handrails for steps should normally maintain a constant height of 900 mm above the nose of the tread, while safety barriers are usually 1.1 m or more.

SAFETY

Openings in barriers may need to be designed so that young children cannot crawl through or get their heads stuck between the railings. Some local regulations specifically require this.

Where particularly large or dangerous changes in level occur, leaning over the balustrades may need to be discouraged. This can be achieved by returning the main rail towards the pedestrian, by setting the balustrade back from the level change, or by using a combination of balustrading and planting to camouflage the height.

Alternatively, the bottom section can be made solid and constructed as a low wall, with a balustrade mounted on top to give a sense of solidity, safety, or privacy.

DETAILING

Tube sections for hand rails should be comfortable to hold with no sharp corners and should allow the hand to run continuously along the length of the rail.

For promenades and waterfronts a wide comfortable top rail may be provided as a leaning rail for viewing.

MATERIALS

Steel and timber are the most common materials. Both are highly adaptable for many locations, both formal and informal, and can be used in combination.

　　　　GENERAL PRINCIPLES

ADAPTABLE FIXING

Fixing details can be made capable of adaptation to a variety of possible situations including fixing to paving and to walls, as well as integration with lighting and other street furniture components.

MODULATION

Long lengths of balustrading should be divided up into separate panels for ease of installation and to accommodate gradual changes of level.

RAILINGS

FENCING

FUNCTION/DEFINITION

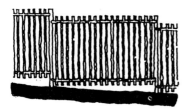

Railings are often used where a physical barrier with some security is required while maintaining visibility or views. Railings and fencing can also be used to indicate a boundary, provide privacy, define a space or provide wind shelter.

TRIP RAIL

Where planting and lawns require protection, pedestrian traffic can be controlled by using a low trip rail about 300 mm high.

MATERIALS

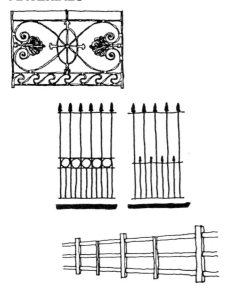

All materials and fixings should be adequately protected against corrosion, especially mild steel.

- *Cast iron*: a traditional material for Victorian railings which is exceptionally durable and corrosive resistant when compared to mild steel. It can also be produced in intricate forms not possible in concrete or steel, and not economically feasible in timber.

- *Steel and aluminium*: these materials are considered to be the best contemporary, light-weight, economical alternatives to cast iron in a city context. Stainless steel should be used in corrosive marine environments, although it is more expensive.

- *Timber*: Wooden railings or fencing may be appropriate for more informal private and public areas. Durability is dependent on the type of timber selected and treatment specification.

COORDINATION

Railings can be used in conjunction with walls to create slot views. Low walls mounted with railings provide a solid base and effective barrier without blocking eye level viewing.

IDENTITY

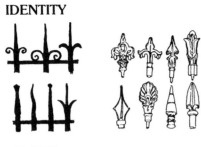

The decorative quality of traditional Victorian railings add a richness to the streetscape. Wrought iron or cast iron may not be feasible but contemporary versions could be designed with standard tube sections, the detailing and decoration varying with each particular area.

HEIGHT

Fencing and railings at eye-level (approximately 1.5 m – 1.7 m high) are visually disturbing and should be avoided. Generally the height should vary according to the level of security required.

TRANSPARENCY

A transparent or solid look to fencing can be created by varying the percentage of solid to void or by selection of colour. Dark colours tend to be more transparent, while light colours appear more opaque.

VISUAL ILLUSION

Visual effects can be created by varying the rhythms of uprights and their thickness, but these should be used with care.

BIKE RACKS

TYPES OF SUPPORT

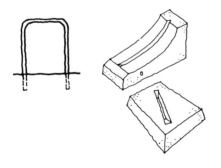

There are two main types of support:

- Vertical: railings are often used to secure bikes where bike racks are not provided. Free-standing racks require a minimum of two vertical elements joined.
- Front wheel: the front wheel only is supported and secured.

Both systems may be designed on a modular or back-to-back basis to provide parking for several bikes at a time.

MATERIALS

Sturdy materials which resist corrosion and vandalism are most commonly used, such as precast concrete, heavy-duty tubular steel hot dip galvanized, or treated timber.

FIXING

Racks may be wall-mounted, surface or below ground fixed. Fixings should be robust to provide the necessary security.

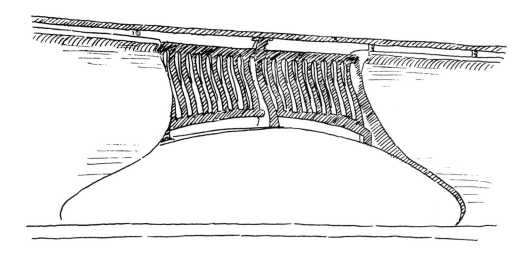

HIROSHIMA, JAPAN
, BRIDGE BALUSTRADE
, SECTIONS OF RAILINGS ALTERNATE
WITH SOLID CONSTRUCTION
, NOTE THE ORGANIC DETAIL AND SLIGHT
RECESS WITH SIGNAGE BELOW

VANCOUVER EXPO '86, CANADA
, RIVERSIDE BALUSTRADE
, GOOD COMBINATION OF A LARGE SECTION
TUBULAR TOP RAIL WITH UPRIGHTS CURVED
LANDWARD AND SMALL SECTION HORIZONTALS
, HAS A NAUTICAL CHARACTER

NIJO · KYOTO · JAPAN
· TIMBER BRIDGE BALUSTRADE
· COPPER STRAP FIXES RAIL
· FIXINGS DESIGNED AS FEATURES

KIYOMIZU · KYOTO · JAPAN
· CORNER DETAIL OF BALUSTRADE
· TIMBER CAPPED WITH COPPER NOW
  WEATHERED GREEN

DAVIS · CALIFORNIA · USA
· LOW PEDESTRIAN BRIDGE RAIL
· DESIGNED WITH CHUNKY SECTIONS
· TOOTHED END TO PLATFORM

GENERAL PRINCIPLES

CHAING MAI · THAILAND
· BRIDGE CONSTRUCTED OF BAMBOO
· WOVEN SPLIT BAMBOO DECK

FISHERMAN'S WHARF · SAN FRANCISCO
· TIMBER BALUSTRADE WITH TILTED TOP
  RAIL FOR LEANING
· ROUGH SAWN TIMBER WITH
  CONSPICUOUS BOLT FIXINGS

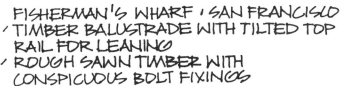

THE MOUNT · EDINBURGH · SCOTLAND
· CAST IRON HAND RAIL
· POSTS WITH LIONS TO RECEIVE THE RAIL

TOKYO , JAPAN
, RAILINGS CONSTRUCTED OF FLAT BARS
TWISTED THROUGH 90° TO MAKE A PATTERN
OF VOID AND SOLID WHEN VIEWED ALONG THE
FENCE

GARE DE LYON , PARIS , FRANCE
, TYPICALLY ORGANIC ART NOUVEAU
DETAIL
, SIGNAGE AND RAILINGS COORDINATED
AND DESIGNED WITH A REAL SENSE
OF ARTISTRY

DANUBE , VIENNA , AUSTRIA
, BEAUTIFULLY DETAILED CAST IRON
RAILINGS WITH WIDE STONE BASE
AND SIMPLE CONTINUOUS TUBULAR
TOP RAIL

RIVERPLACE ' MINNEAPOLIS ' USA
' BALUSTRADE WELL COORDINATED WITH
  PLANTER HEIGHT TO MAINTAIN CONTINUITY
' A SIMPLE WELL CONCEIVED DETAIL

TOKYO ' JAPAN
' RAILINGS DESIGNED TO PROTECT PLANTING
' WELDED CIRCULAR TOP DETAIL MAKES AN
  OTHERWISE STRAIGHT FORWARD DESIGN
  QUITE DECORATIVE

RED CROSS BUILDING , TOKYO , JAPAN
' STONE WALL BASE
' LARGE PANELS WITH TREE PATTERN

IIDABASHI ' TOKYO ' JAPAN
' BRIDGE BALUSTRADE
' SIMPLE FRAMEWORK WITH
  DECORATIVE PANELS
' ALL ONE COLOUR : GUN METAL

MATJIESFONTEIN · SOUTH AFRICA
· FAT · RENDERED PIERS WITH A LOW
WALL IN BETWEEN SUPPORTING
FINE DECORATIVE RAILINGS
· EFFECTIVE CONTRAST OF BOLD AND
INTRICATE DETAILING

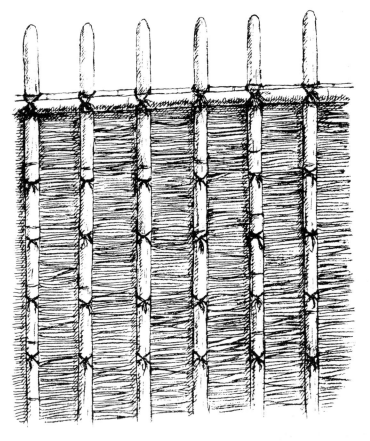

KYOTO · JAPAN
· EXQUISITE BAMBOO FENCE
· UPRIGHTS AND RAIL TIED
 TOGETHER
· PANELS OF FINE WOVEN
 BRANCHES

KYOTO · JAPAN
· DETAIL OF A TYPICAL FENCE PANEL
· A FINE EXAMPLE OF CRAFTSMANSHIP

KYOTO · JAPAN
· BAMBOO FENCE HELD TOGETHER WITH
 STRING
· SPLIT BAMBOO FORMS A LATTICE

KYOTO · JAPAN
BUNDLES OF BAMBOO FORM
A LOW GARDEN FENCE OVER
A STONE EDGING

NARA · JAPAN
· LOW RAIL CONNECTION IN BAMBOO
· SPLIT BAMBOO AND STRING FIXING

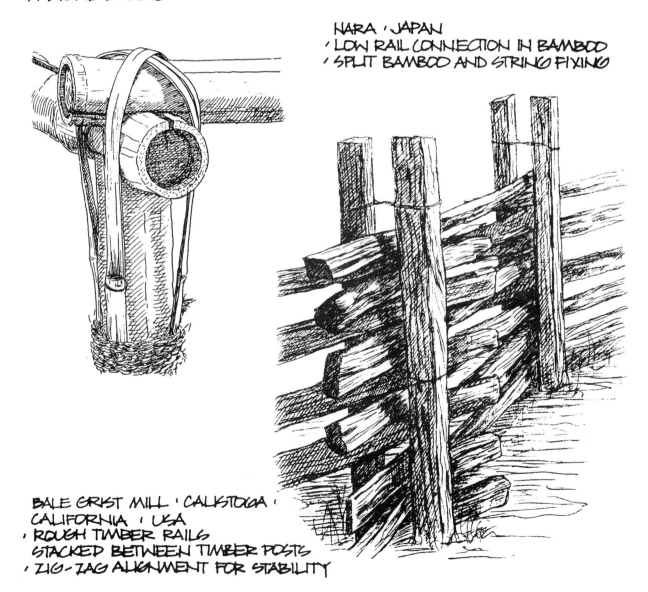

BALE GRIST MILL · CALISTOGA ·
CALIFORNIA · USA
· ROUGH TIMBER RAILS
STACKED BETWEEN TIMBER POSTS
· ZIG-ZAG ALIGNMENT FOR STABILITY

TSUKUBA · JAPAN
· CYCLE RACK USING FLAT SECTION
  STEEL ALL BOLTED TO THE PAVING
· EFFECTIVE SUPPORT SYSTEM

NEW YORK · USA
· SIMPLE AND EFFECTIVE BIKE RACK

EXPO '86 · VANCOUVER · CANADA
· BIKE STAND WITH A HUNG TOP BIKE
  WHEEL FIX
· TUBULAR STEEL STRUCTURE BOLTED
  TO PAVING

Walls

Walls

SPACE DEFINITION

Walls provide a visual and physical barrier, mainly used to define private and semi-private areas. They can be integrated with other hard landscape areas such as:

- Raised planters.
- Changes of level.
- Seating/wall-mounted benches.
- Shelters and kiosks.

RETAINING WALL TREATMENT

Low walls are less obtrusive visually. They may be used as a device to increase soil depths for planting on roof structures. High retaining walls can be divided into terraces and softened with planting or stepped to provide form seating opportunities.

FREESTANDING WALL TREATMENT

Where views need to be maintained, low walls should be used to define areas of activity. Low walls may be designed with an appropriate coping height and material to double as a seat.

High walls should generally be integrated into the design of structures and buildings rather than used as freestanding elements. Boundary walls and those designed as features are obvious exceptions.

High walls can form effective enclosure and can be articulated as a sculptural form to channel or block views, to carry particular textures or murals, or to act as a neutral backdrop to contain the view to a single focus.

MATERIALS

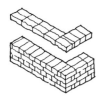 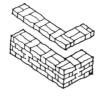

Walls should be constructed with materials which complement the surrounding hard landscaping and architecture.

Materials should be selected with an eye to weathering and corrosion, the most common being brick, stone and concrete. There are an infinite number of coursing and pointing possibilities, as well as textured finishes such as exposed aggregate, terrazzo and bush-hammered techniques.

GENERAL PRINCIPLES

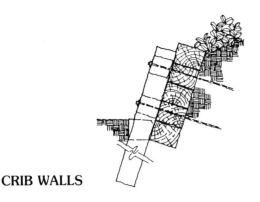

Timber is particularly unobtrusive when associated with planting. Half logs, used railway sleepers are commonly used for low retaining walls anchored back using 'dead men' or earth anchors for stability. The specification and treatment of such timber should be thoroughly researched to ensure longevity of the structure.

CRIB WALLS

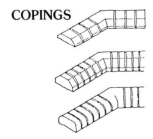

Timber or concrete crib walls are open frameworks constructed by stacking precast, interlocking units filled with free draining material. Due to the open nature of the structure planting pockets may be incorporated which can help to reduce the visual impact of this type of large retaining wall.

GABIONS

Gabions, or stone filled wire baskets, are not generally used in an urban context because of their rough appearance. They are suitable for the control of erosion on river and roadway cuttings and are made of heavy-duty wire cages filled with stone. The inherent mass of the wall makes an economical and extremely erosion resistant solution.

FOUNDATIONS

Footings should be adequately deep to prevent damage by frost. Foundation size and shape will depend upon wall thickness, material, height and whether the structure is retaining or freestanding.

EXPANSION JOINTS

Long walls, especially those constructed of brick or concrete will require expansion joints to prevent cracking by allowing the structure to expand and contract. The joints should be incorporated carefully so as not to reduce the integral strength of the wall overall.

STABILITY

The stability of high freestanding walls can either be achieved by curving or stepping the wall, by using buttresses or varying the thickness of the wall from top to bottom.

COPINGS

The function of a coping is to shed the water to either side of the wall to prevent moisture absorption and freeze–thaw action from above. The design may be a small flush detail in the same material as the wall or it may be designed with a large, almost roof-like, coping detailed relate as part of a larger building vocabulary. The coping of a low wall may double as a seat by designing it to the right height, width and edge detail for comfort.

EFFLORESCENCE

Efflorescence is the precipitation of salts caused by moisture absorption out of or through materials such as brick and concrete. The results may look unsightly and be the cause of characteristic streaking on concrete or white bloom on brickwork. This can be prevented by careful selection of materials, and in the case of retaining walls, by waterproofing the back of the wall with an applied liquid or sheet sealant material.

DRAINAGE

 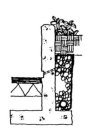

Dry stone and crib walls are pervious structures allowing water to seep through. Other impervious retaining structures will require some form of drainage to prevent the accumulation of ground water pressure behind the wall. This usually takes the form of both a piped drain and weep holes at the base of the wall.

TOKYO · JAPAN
· STONE WALL OF MASSIVE
 PROPORTIONS
· STRONG CORNER CONSTRUCTION

TSUKUBA SCIENCE CITY · JAPAN
· BEAUTIFULLY GRADED WALL
· FROM ROUGH HEWN TO DRESSED
 STONE AND FROM RANDOM TO
 COURSED CONSTRUCTION

RYOAN-JI · KYOTO · JAPAN
· STRONG ENCLOSING ELEMENT TO THE
  DRY STONE GARDEN
· RENDERED WALL WEATHERED INTO
  BEAUTIFUL ABSTRACT PATTERNS

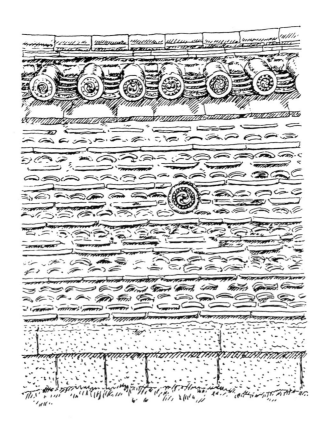

DAITOKUJI · KYOTO · JAPAN
· SECTION OF A TEMPLE WALL
· BUSH HAMMERED GRANITE BASE
· COURSED RANDOM TILE MAIN SECTION
· TILES FORM A ROOF LIKE COPING

U.C. SANTA CRUZ · CALIFORNIA · USA
- WALLS TREATED AS SCULPTURAL
  SEPARATING ELEMENTS
- HOLES ARE CUT AND CREATE SEAT
  HEIGHT LEDGES

U.C. SANTA CRUZ · CALIFORNIA · USA
- WALLS FORM OUTDOOR SCREENS
- THEY FRAME SELECTED VIEWS AND
  CREATE A SENSE OF ENCLOSURE
- THESE WALLS ARE A PART OF THE
  SAME ARCHITECTURAL VOCABULARY
  AS ADJACENT BUILDINGS

WALLS   115

BELVEDERE · VIENNA · AUSTRIA
· HEDGE AS A LIVING WALL
· TREES GROWN THROUGH FOR A
  HIGH CANOPY
· PRECISELY CLIPPED

SISSINGHURST · KENT · UK
· COMBINATION OF WALLS AND HEDGES
  TO ENCLOSE GARDEN SPACES

GENERAL PRINCIPLES

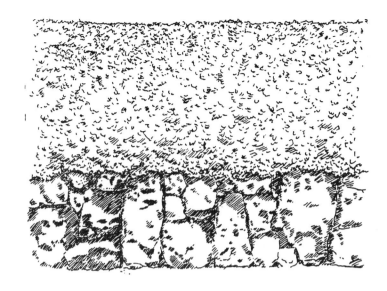

TOFUKUJI · KYOTO · JAPAN
· LOW DRY STONE WALL GIVEN
  HEIGHT WITH HEDGE PLANTING

DAISEN - IN · KYOTO · JAPAN
· TYPICAL JAPANESE PICTURE WINDOW
  TECHNIQUE IN AN EXTERNAL WALL
· THESE WINDOWS CREATE THE LINKING
  ELEMENT BETWEEN OUTDOOR ROOMS

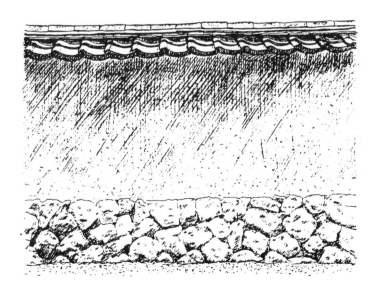

KYOTO · JAPAN
· DRY STONE RANDOM COURSE WALL BASE
· RENDERED UPPER WALL
· COPING TREATED AS A SMALL ROOF

CHAING MAI ' THAILAND
' LOW ' FAT AND RENDERED WALL
AROUND A SHRINE
' HOLES PIERCED THROUGH AND
TOP ARTICULATED

STRANDFONTEIN ' RSA
' BLOCKWORK WALL WITH AN ORGANIC
WAVING TOP TO SUIT THE BEACH
LOCATION

Gateways
Gates

Gateways
Gates

FUNCTION

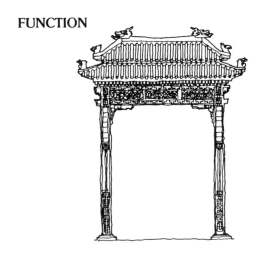

Gateways may form strong focal attractions. They may be freestanding and architecturally impressive, to herald the entrance to a park, and to create a sense of arrival and orientation.

Gateways may perform several other functions:

- They may incorporate paying kiosks for entrance control or for vending.
- They may frame a view, or part of a view as a clue to what lies beyond.
- They may enhance the spacial qualities of 'hereness and thereness' (Cullen) within an otherwise open space.

OPENING

Gates should have a minimum clear opening of 800 mm.

An open gate should not obstruct any adjacent walkways.

HEIGHT

The top of a gate may not necessarily be the same height as the rest of the barrier. A gate which is higher or lower tends to visually emphasise the point of entry.

TRANSPARENCY

The point of entry may be further emphasisied by the change of material and degree of transparency between the gate and the rest of the barrier. A cast-iron gate in a high solid brick wall will tend to invite you toward the gate to view beyond.

MOULINS · FRANCE
· DECORATIVE IRONWORK TO
GATEWAY WITH CENTRAL HIGH
POINT AND SWIRLING PATTERNS

THE BELVEDERE · VIENNA · AUSTRIA
· ORNATE CAST IRON WORK FORMS A
GATEWAY THROUGH TO FORMAL GARDENS
· CARVED STONE PIERS FRAME THE GATE

NANZENJI · KYOTO · JAPAN.
· GARDEN WALL GATEWAY INVITES YOU THROUGH
· TIERED ROOF OVER OPENING IDENTIFIES
  AND EMPHASISES ITS POSITION

GOVERNMENT AVENUE · CAPE TOWN
· RENDERED AND WHITEWASHED GATEWAY
  DESIGNED WITH HEAVY RUSTICATED PROPORTIONS
· CONTRASTING DELICATE IRONWORK

TOKYO · JAPAN
· PARK GATEWAY ON AN ENORMOUS SCALE
· VAST TUBULAR STEEL SECTIONS

KYOTO · JAPAN
· BAMBOO FENCE AND GATE
· GATE DESIGNED WITH VOIDS SO THAT
  A HINT OF WHAT LIES BEYOND IS GIVEN

MOUNT NELSON · CAPE TOWN · RSA
· NEO CLASSICAL VEHICULAR GATEWAY
· CREATES AN IMPOSING SENSE OF ENTRY

STRANDFONTEIN · RSA
· COASTAL DEVELOPMENT TAKES ON A
  HUMOROUS WAVE MOTIF WITH AN INFORMAL
  ASYMMETRICAL SILHOUETTE

Lighting

Lighting

COORDINATED SUPPORTS

A standard system of supports should be used for all lamp-posts in any particular area. These in turn should be co-ordinated with bin and signage supports to minimise the number of poles.

SELECTION AND SITING

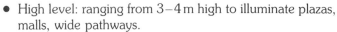

The level and type of lighting should express the function and character of an area. Pedestrian lighting can be put broadly into two categories, amenity and decorative.

AMENITY:

- High level: ranging from 3–4 m high to illuminate plazas, malls, wide pathways.
- Low level: bollard lights for more intimate lighting of narrow pathways, seating, eating or planting areas.
- Bulk-head: alongside steps and ramps where projecting fittings or pole supports would obtrude.

DECORATIVE:

- Floodlighting: illumination of special buildings, monuments, fountains or planting, which can either be pole-mounted, wall-mounted or low-level and angled.
- Festive lighting: multiple lights and special effects for festive occasions.

WALL-MOUNTED

Where it is desirable for the number of vertical elements to be minimised, light fittings can be mounted to walls, columns and buildings; for example, in narrow lanes.

ADAPTABLE FIXING

Fixings should be adaptable so that any one light fitting can be mounted or clustered in several different ways, and combined with structures and signage.

MATERIALS

Low maintenance materials are preferable. Any metal should be treated appropriately against corrosion. Stainless steel and a marine quality aluminium should be considered in coastal areas.

GENERAL PRINCIPLES

LIGHTING ATMOSPHERE

The colour and illumination level should be carefully selected. A warm light suitable for pedestrian areas can be achieved by using a high-pressure sodium lamp. More intimate or festive lighting can be created with lower level incandescent lamps, but these require more frequent maintenance.

The most common types of illumination include:

- *Incandescent*: suitable for small areas giving a high intensity light source. A warm twinkling light. No ballast required.
- *Tungsten halogen*: tubular lamp combining a tungsten filament with halogen gas. Low voltage compact types are available providing a high level of illumination for low energy consumption. Transformer required for a 12-volt supply.
- *Compact fluorescent*: suitable for lighting large areas with a low intensity light. Gives a cool illumination and requires a ballast.
- *Mercury vapour*: suitable for illuminating large areas with a cool high intensity light. Usually mounted above 4 m high. Requires a ballast. May render false colours.
- *Metal halide*: a warm white or white light that provides a high intensity 'wash' suitable for floodlighting buildings or illuminating planting. Ballast required.
- *High-pressure sodium*: a warm light for lighting large areas with a low intensity illumination usually associated with street lighting. Requires a ballast. The yellow light quality falsely renders certain colours.
- *Low-pressure sodium*: a low wattage version of high-pressure sodium, with a more gentle yellow or warm colour appearance. Both high and low pressure types are very energy efficient. Ballast required.
- *Reflective*: where the light source is dependent and controlled by the viewer, and is therefore only illuminated when needed. Usually this type is used for roadway signage and road lane indication.

Areas where there may be activities at night may require a higher than usual illumination with special lighting for events. Light levels should vary to emphasise entrances, focusses and special features.

HISTORIC AREAS

Simple contemporary fixtures reflecting modern lighting requirements should be selected. Alternatively, many reproduction Victorian fittings are available which have been adapted to take all types of light source.

COASTAL LOCATION

Factors to consider in the design for coastal areas are:

- Windloading if the fittings are freestanding.
- Corrosion of support and fittings.
- Salt crusting of luminaire.
- Seagull droppings.

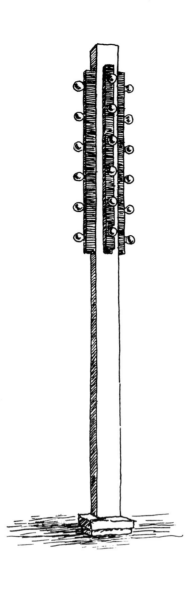

SAN FRANCISCO · USA
· POLE DESIGNED AS A LUMINAIRE
· FOUR SIDED MOUNTING OF
  INCANDESCENT BULBS IN STRIPS OF SIX
· COMBINES A STRONG STRUCTURE WITH
  A DELICATE LIGHTING SOLUTION

HARBOR PLACE · BOSTON · USA
· LARGE GLASS LANTERN WITH PROTECTIVE
  CAGE USING FLAT SECTION STEEL IN BLACK
· IN CHARACTER WITH HARBOUR LOCATION

GENERAL PRINCIPLES

MILAN · ITALY
· CYLINDRICAL STONE BASE
· TUBULAR STEEL 'BRANCH LIKE' SUPPORTS
· POLYCARBONATE LUMINAIRE

CHRISTIAN SCIENCE CENTER · BOSTON
· CLUSTER OF LIGHTS
· SUPPORT SYSTEM IN A CRUCIFIX FORM
· RAISED CONCRETE BASE WITH INTEGRAL
  MOWING EDGE DETAIL

MILAN · ITALY
· RUSTICATED STONE BASE
· CLUSTER OF LIGHTS ON
  BRANCHING TUBULAR SUPPORTS

SEATTLE · WASHINGTON · USA
· LARGE WALL MOUNTED GAS LAMP
· SIMPLE BRACKET SUPPORT

OXFORD · ENGLAND
· TOP OF WALL FIXING
· GLASS SPHERE
· DELICATE IRONWORK

OXFORD · ENGLAND
· WALL MOUNTED LANTERN
· FINE TWISTED WROUGHT IRONWORK

AMALFI · ITALY
· WATERFRONT LIGHT STANDARDS
· CLUSTERS OF FOUR FITTINGS
· TWINKLING INCANDESCENT LIGHT

SCIENCE MUSEUM · HAMMAMTSU · JAPAN
· PEDESTRIAN AND VEHICULAR LIGHTING
  COMBINED
· SIMPLE AND UNCLUTTERED DESIGN
· COLOURS : WHITE SUPPORTS WITH DARK GREY
  SHADES

IIDABASHI DISTRICT · TOKYO · JAPAN
· KERB SIDE STREET LIGHTING
· SMALLER LANTERN HUNG OVER SIDEWALK
· LARGER LANTERN SUPPORTED HIGH OVER
  STREET

STANFORD UNIVERSITY · CALIFORNIA
· CLUSTER LIGHTING
· FIVE OPAQUE SPHERES 'HELD' WITH
  DECORATIVE FIXINGS

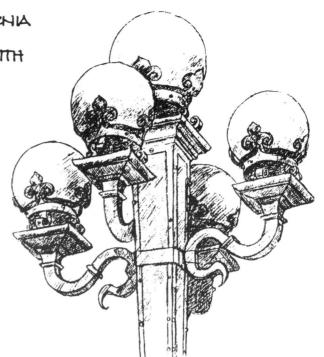

NATURAL HISTORY MUSEUM AND PLANETARIUM
CAPE TOWN · RSA
· CUSTOM MADE SUPPORT AND SPHERE CRADLE
· DESIGN RESPONDS TO THE ARCHITECTURAL
  CONTEXT AND FUNCTION

VANCOUVER · CANADA
· WALL MOUNTED CAST IRON FITTING WITH
  OPAQUE LUMINAIRE
· SWITCH GEAR BOX CONSPICUOUS BUT
  INOFFENSIVE

PARIS / FRANCE
/ ILLUMINATED RED LETTERING
/ OPAQUE SPHERE
/ GENERAL PAINT COLOUR ; BOTTLE GREEN

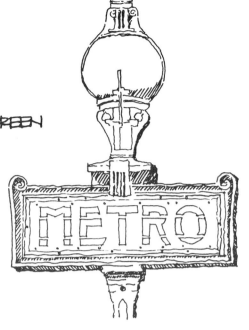

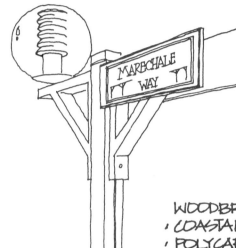

WOODBRIDGE ISLAND · CAPE TOWN
/ COASTAL SCHEME
/ POLYCARBONATE HIGH PRESSURE SODIUM LAMP
/ SCREENED ALUMINIUM SIGN
/ TIMBER SUPPORT BRACKETS AND POST

HOUSES OF PARLIAMENT · CAPE TOWN
/ CAST IRON AND GLASS
/ INCANDESCENT LAMPS MOUNTED ON PILLARS

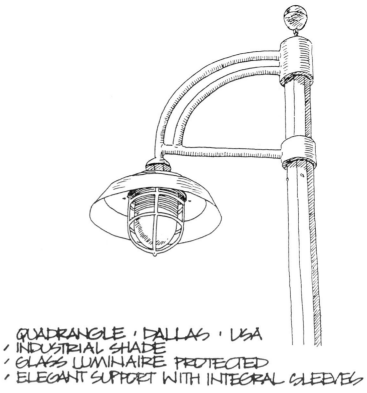

QUADRANGLE · DALLAS · USA
, INDUSTRIAL SHADE
, GLASS LUMINAIRE PROTECTED
, ELEGANT SUPPORT WITH INTEGRAL SLEEVES

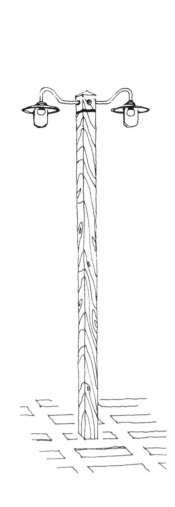

SURREY DOCKS · LONDON
, TIMBER POST WITH
  INDUSTRIAL TYPE FITTING
, WELL DETAILED LIGHTING
  SUPPORT ARMS

QUADRANGLE · DALLAS · TEXAS
, DOUBLE VERSION FOR ILLUMINATING
  CAR PARK AND SIDEWALK

SAN FRANCISCO , USA
' LIGHT FITTINGS DESIGNED TO ENHANCE THE
CHINESE QUARTER
' COLOURS : CHINESE RED WITH GOLD DRAGON
AND ORNAMENTATION
' OPAQUE GLASS

TEMPLE OF THE EMERALD BUDDHA '
BANGKOK ' THAILAND
' GILT EDGED CRANE - LIKE BIRD
POISED FOR FLIGHT AND CARRYING
LUMINAIRE
' PERFECT TEMPLE LIGHTING

LIGHTING

GHIRADELLI SQUARE · SAN FRANCISCO
, SPHERICAL SUPPORT FOR A MASS
  OF TINY INCANDESCENT BULBS
, TWINKLING EFFECT AT NIGHT

CENTRAL PARK , NEW YORK
, ELEGANT OPAQUE GLASS LANTERN
, DESIGN ; OLMSTEAD
, LEAFY DETAIL WITH AN ACORN ON THE TOP

NIKKO , JAPAN
, SHRINE POLE MOUNTED LUMINAIRE.
, TIMBER POLE TOP DETAIL PAINTED
  CHINESE RED

ELM STREET · DALLAS · USA
· POLES FLUTED WITH HEAVY BASE DETAIL
· LUMINAIRES MOULDED

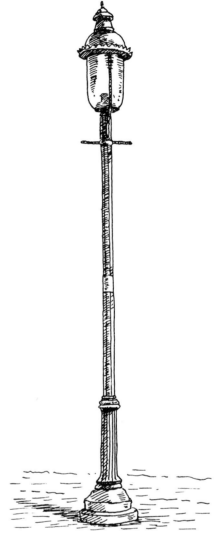

MINNEAPOLIS · USA
· ELEGANT POLE AND LUMINAIRE
DESIGN

CHAING MAI · THAILAND
· SIMPLE POLE AND SPHERE DECORATED
TO GIVE A SENSE OF LOCATION

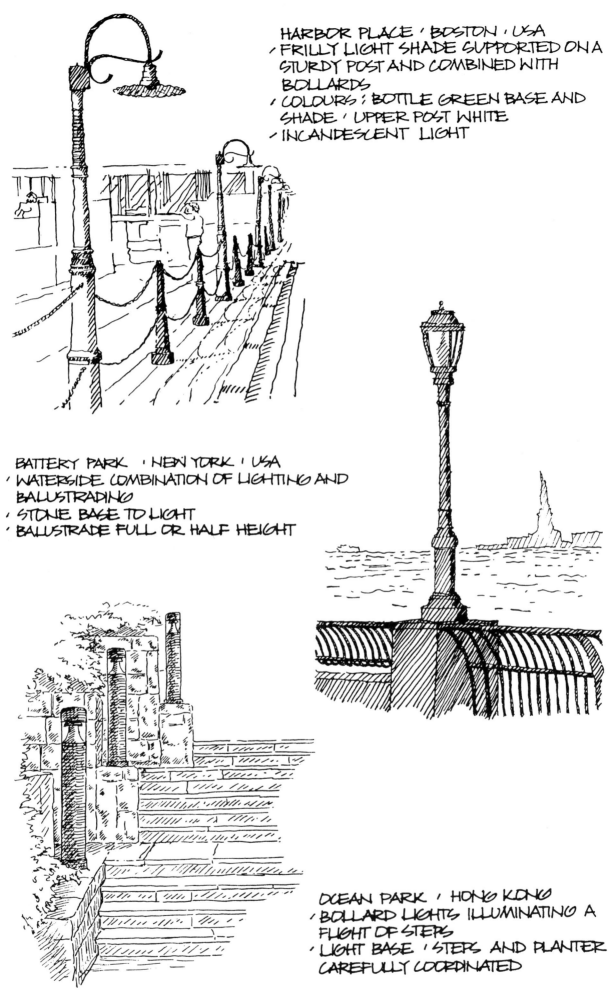

HARBOR PLACE · BOSTON · USA
· FRILLY LIGHT SHADE SUPPORTED ON A
  STURDY POST AND COMBINED WITH
  BOLLARDS
· COLOURS : BOTTLE GREEN BASE AND
  SHADE · UPPER POST WHITE
· INCANDESCENT LIGHT

BATTERY PARK · NEW YORK · USA
· WATERSIDE COMBINATION OF LIGHTING AND
  BALUSTRADING
· STONE BASE TO LIGHT
· BALUSTRADE FULL OR HALF HEIGHT

OCEAN PARK · HONG KONG
· BOLLARD LIGHTS ILLUMINATING A
  FLIGHT OF STEPS
· LIGHT BASE · STEPS AND PLANTER
  CAREFULLY COORDINATED

OXFORD · ENGLAND
· OLD GAS LAMP
· CIRCULAR CAST IRON POST WITH
  UNUSUAL SQUAT SQUARE SECTION BASE

SMITHSONIAN, WASHINGTON D.C.
· MALL HIGH MAST LIGHTING WITH A
  LARGE LANTERN
· ARCHITECTURAL GRAPHICS REPRESENT
  DIFFERENT MUSEUMS

Signage
Banners

Signage
Banners

RATIONALISATION

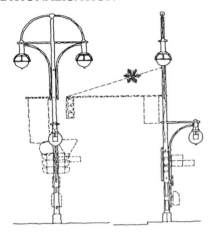

Signage should be rationalised to minimise the clutter of poles. Signs can also be fixed to walls and buildings to reduce the number of supports, or combined on to one pole as part of a structure which might carry other street furniture components.

The height, size and shape of signs should be rationalised to maximise legibility and give a particular character to an area. A consistent horizontal relationship of signs can help create a tidier visual appearance.

Local authorities and large companies may be well advised to produce a special manual to control the 'house style' and application of signs and notices.

SITING OF SIGNS

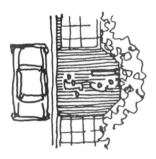

Signage should not be unnecessarily obtrusive. The visual environment will affect sign legibility and signs mounted in front of planting or against a building can be distinguished from the background by contrast in texture. Untidy silhouette-effects against the sky should be avoided. Low signs are less obtrusive and feel more in scale with pedestrian areas.

Pedestrian information boards should be sited in positions where people can pause without obstructing other pedestrians.

Signs can be fixed to walls and buildings to avoid exposing the rear view of a signboard.

IMAGEABILITY

The way that signage is treated in the streetscape will depend on imageability. Signage should be appropriate to the architectural surroundings and combine aesthetics and function.

PHYSICAL FACTORS

Factors to be considered in the design of signage:

- The field of vision, which is 60°.
- Reading rate or speed particularly when in a moving vehicle.
- Average eye levels: 1.7 m when standing, 1.3 m when sitting, 1.4 m in a car.

SIGNAGE FUNCTIONS

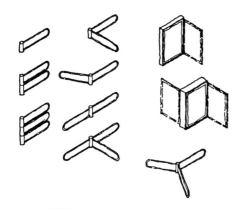

Signs may be divided into the following categories:

- *Directional*: routes.
- *Identification*: buildings, squares and parks.
- *Traffic control*: roads and parking signs.
- *Information*: historical, locational, events.
- *Heraldry*: banners, flags, murals, emblems, logos.

A family of signs may be considered relating to a specific area and based on shape, colour and fixing.

GRAPHICS

The graphics for each type should reflect user's requirements:

- *Vehicles*: legibility at speed and from a distance with bold and simple sans serif typeface; minimum height 100 mm, or 25 mm for every 7.5 m distance from the sign with the number of items limited to between six and ten.
- *Pedestrians*: more detailed information can be conveyed with smaller and more decorative typefaces.

Those signs which are legally enforceable should comply with traffic regulation standards.

International standards should be used for traffic and safety signage, while most other signage can be customised to fit in with the character or design concept of an area.

Non-functional and decorative graphics may be used simply to enhance an architectural or landscape project. Symbols, except where these are universally understood, should not be used without supporting explanatory information.

GRAPHICS IMAGEABILITY

The number of typefaces used should be kept to a minimum.

Typefaces should be appropriate in terms of the character of the area and function:

abcdefghijklmnopqrstuvwxyz
ABCDEFGHIJKLMNOPQRSTUVWXYZ

abcdefghijklmnopqrstuvwxyz
ABCDEFGHIJKLMNOPQRSTUVWXYZ

abcdefghijklmnopqrstuvwxyz
ABCDEFGHIJKLMNOPQRSTUVWXYZ

- In and around an airport, for example, the function of rapid communications is most important.
- For transportation uncomplicated typefaces should be specified; sans serif, such as 'Helvetica', or 'Univers'.
- Historic or conservation areas may adopt a classical typeface such as 'Times New Roman'.
- Recreational areas may require lettering which fits a theme and can be more adventurous and informal.

The shape and size of a sign will be determined by the size of the lettering and its location.

TEXT/COPY

When designing the copy for signs, the following considerations should be borne in mind:

- Spacing of lettering.
- Spacing between lines.
- The space or dimension from baseline to baseline of copy.
- Position of symbols or logos.
- Margins.
- Whether the copy is centred or justified.
- The use of either upper- and/or lower-case.

MATERIALS

Signs may be fabricated from a number of materials including sheet metal, bronze, aluminium, timber, stone, concrete, acrylic plastic, fibreglass.

If the copy is an integral part of the sign, rather than applied, maintenance will generally be reduced.

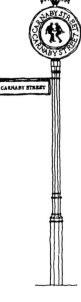

LOGOS AND EMBLEMS

A logo or emblem can help to indentify each particular district of a city. Logos can be used in conjunction with directional signs, paving, flags, and information boards to reinforce a message. They may not be able to stand on their own but can be particularly useful as signals at a distance.

Logos should be legible, adaptable for application in various locations and materials, and should relate to their associated graphics.

Care should be taken in creating new symbols as many have been standardised internationally.

BANNERS AND FLAGS

FUNCTION

Banners and flags add movement, colour and a festive air to the streetscape. They help to identify important buildings or places, and can also be used for information or advertising. They may be purely decorative and be designed by artists.

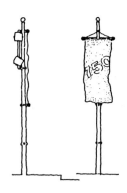

SHAPE

As a general rule banners hang vertically. Flags are generally rectangular and flow horizontally, they may however also be made to hang vertically from a parapet, for instance.

GENERAL PRINCIPLES

FIXING

Wind loading causes the greatest damage to banners and flags. To minimise maintenance the following factors should be considered:

- Type of banner or flag fabric.
- Perforating the fabric.
- Height and length of the banner or flag.
- Fixing of fabric: top and bottom, top only, top with loose bottom fixing.

Banners should not hang too low on pedestrian routes because of obstruction and the risk of vandalism.

NON-GRAPHIC SIGNS

In some cases the proliferation of signs can be minimised by using non-graphic symbols such as:

- Painted lines.
- Rumble strips (textured paving).
- Bollards.

Signs may also be avoided simply by careful planning of particular environments, based on an analysis and an understanding of the users' requirements and habits.

U.C. SANTA CRUZ · CALIFORNIA
· TIMBER SIGN
· LETTERING CARVED AND PAINTED WHITE
· SIMPLE POST AND PLANK CONSTRUCTION

HONG KONG
· ADVERTISING STAND WITH FAR MORE
OF A SENSE OF ARCHITECTURE AND
CULTURE THAN MOST OF THE SURROUDING
HOUSING DEVELOPMENT

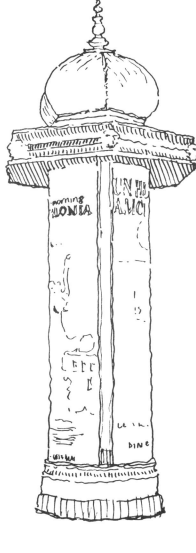

VIENNA · AUSTRIA
· BEAUTIFULLY DETAILED AND IMPOSING
AD' STANDS ARE OF SUCH A SCALE AND
SO PROLIFIC THAT THEY BECOME PIECES
OF STREETSCAPE ARCHITECTURE

PARIS / FRANCE
· ADVERTISING STANDS
· MOORISH ARCHITECTURAL DETAIL
· GOOD SCALE FOR THE PARIS STREETSCAPE

SOUTH STREET SEAPORT · NEW YORK
· TUBULAR SUPPORTS TAPERED
· FISH SCULPTURE MOTIF
· GOOD CLEAR GRAPHICS

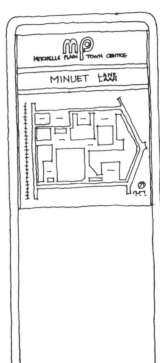

MITCHELLS PLAIN · CAPE TOWN · RSA
· INFORMATION SIGN WITH NEAT
FRAMING SUPPORT SYSTEM

MINNEAPOLIS · USA
· CAST IRON DECORATIVE COLUMNAR
SUPPORTS
· SIGN WITH PROJECTING GRAPHICS

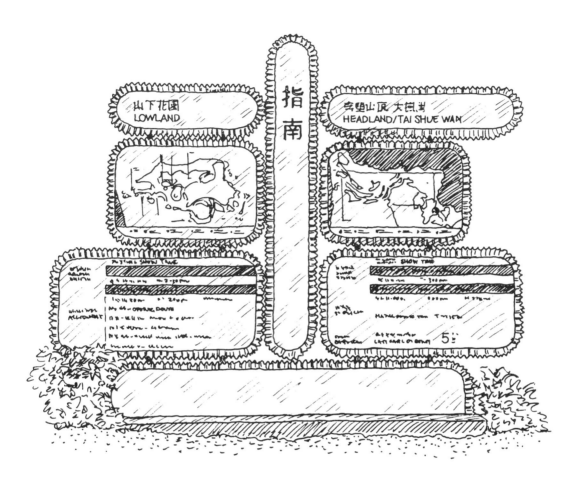

OCEAN PARK · HONG KONG
· SERRATED INTERLOCKING SIGNS
· ORIENTATION MAPS AND OPENING TIMES/RATES
· COLOUR: SEA BLUE EDGING, LIGHT BLUE SIGNS

THE MALL , WASHINGTON D,C,
, INFORMATION STAND WITH MAPS AND
LOCATION KEY
, CANOPY TO PROTECT THE STRUCTURE
AND THE VIEWER FROM THE WEATHER

EXPO' 86 , VANCOUVER , CANADA
, STRETCHED FABRIC PANELS BACK
LIT AND COLOUR COORDINATED
, TUBULAR ALUMINIUM STRUCTURE

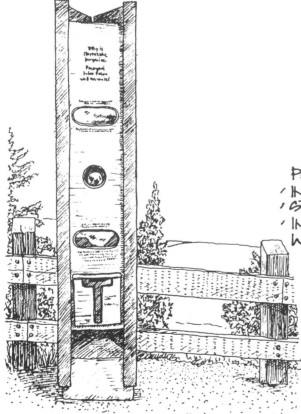

PEYTO LAKE , ALBERTA , CANADA
, INFORMATION SIGN
, STEEL WITH A CONCRETE BASE
, INCORPORATING CENTRAL PEEP HOLE
WITH MAP AND POCKET FOR LEAFLETS

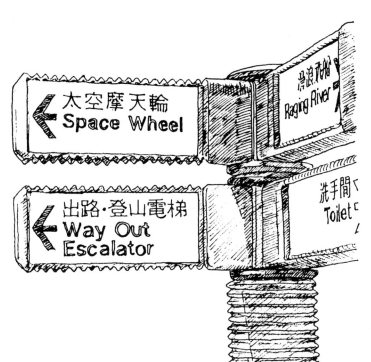

OCEAN PARK · HONG KONG
· ILLUMINATED SIGNS
· CORRUGATED PVC SUPPORT

CORNWALL · ENGLAND
· CAST IRON SIGNS WITH INTEGRAL
SLEEVES TO STACK OVER POST

TSUKUBA · NEAR TOKYO · JAPAN
· STAINLESS STEEL 'CUT OUT' SIGNAGE USING
FLAT SECTIONS
· SIGN WALL FIXED AND CANTILEVERED

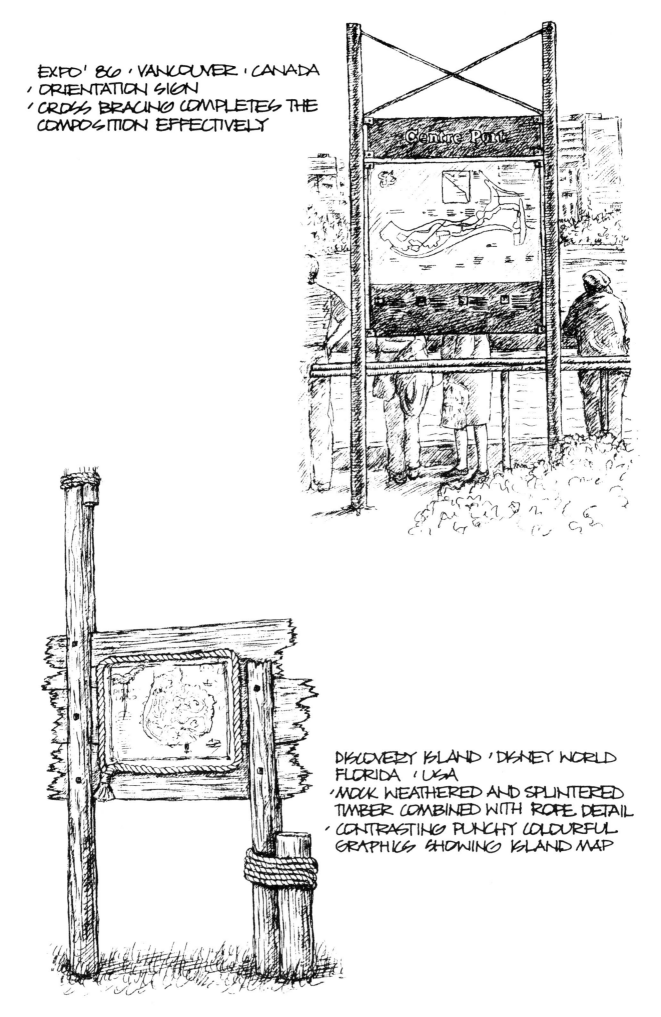

EXPO' 86 · VANCOUVER · CANADA
· ORIENTATION SIGN
· CROSS BRACING COMPLETES THE
  COMPOSITION EFFECTIVELY

DISCOVERY ISLAND · DISNEY WORLD
FLORIDA · USA
· MOCK WEATHERED AND SPLINTERED
  TIMBER COMBINED WITH ROPE DETAIL
· CONTRASTING PUNCHY COLOURFUL
  GRAPHICS SHOWING ISLAND MAP

EXPO' 86 · VANCOUVER · CANADA

TOKYO, JAPAN.
, SIGN INSET INTO WALL
, A SOPHISTICATED COMBINATION OF POLISHED
GRANITE AND OFF SHUTTER CONCRETE

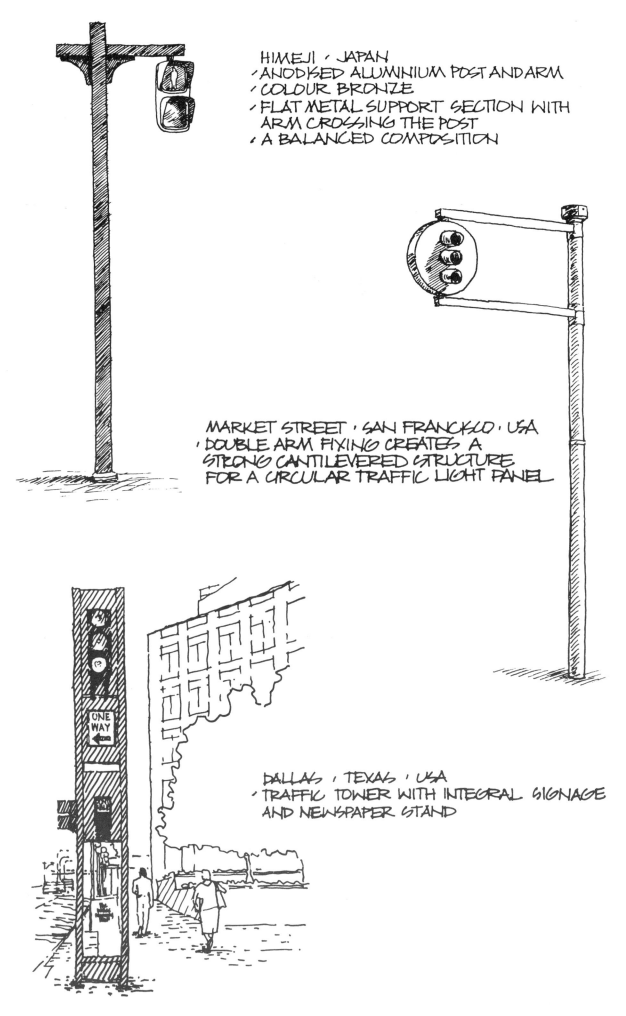

HIMEJI · JAPAN
· ANODISED ALUMINIUM POST AND ARM
· COLOUR BRONZE
· FLAT METAL SUPPORT SECTION WITH
  ARM CROSSING THE POST
· A BALANCED COMPOSITION

MARKET STREET · SAN FRANCISCO · USA
· DOUBLE ARM FIXING CREATES A
  STRONG CANTILEVERED STRUCTURE
  FOR A CIRCULAR TRAFFIC LIGHT PANEL

DALLAS · TEXAS · USA
· TRAFFIC TOWER WITH INTEGRAL SIGNAGE
  AND NEWSPAPER STAND

ONE
WAY

MARKET STREET · SAN FRANCISCO
· NEAT COMBINATION OF TRAFFIC
LIGHTS AND SIGNS

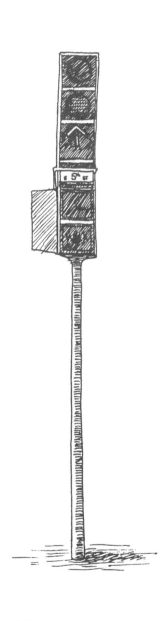

NICOLLET MALL · MINNEAPOLIS · USA
· COMBINED TRAFFIC AND STREET
SIGNAGE STACKED LIKE A TOTEM POLE

SEA RANCH · CALIFORNIA
· LOW PROFILE FOOTPATH SIGNAGE
· TIMBER POST WITH SCREENED
ALUMINIUM SIGNS

FISHERMAN'S WHARF , SAN FRANCISCO
, TIMBER FLAG POLES EACH CARRYING
   MANY FLAGS
, GOOD COLOURFUL IMPACT

DALLAS · TEXAS · USA
· VAST FLAGPOLES TAPERING DRAMATICALLY
· ENORMOUS FLAGS CLOSELY SPACED

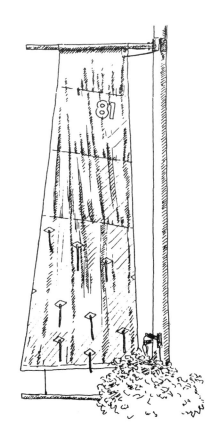

SEATTLE · WASHINGTON · USA
· BANNER WITH TASSLES
· POLE ALSO CARRIES HANGING BASKETS

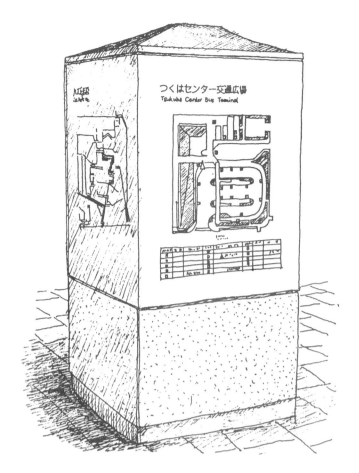

TSUKUBA CENTRE · NEAR TOKYO · JAPAN
· SIGN SHOWING TERMINAL AND TIMETABLE
· CONCRETE BASE
· SCREENED ALUMINIUM SIGN

FOREST OF DEAN · GLOUCESTERSHIRE ·
ENGLAND
· STONE CONSTRUCTION WITH RECESS TO
TAKE MAP AND INFORMATION BOARD

GENERAL PRINCIPLES

Shelters
Canopies
Structures

Shelters
Canopies
Structures

SHELTERS

FUNCTION

Shelters may serve as permanent, long-term or temporary structures:

- *Permanent*: may include colonnades, covered walkways, *porte-cochères*.
- *Long term*: bus stops, kiosks, telephone booths.
- *Temporary*: market stalls, cafe umberellas.

Shelters are required primarily to provide for the pedestrian refuge and protection from the elements.

In all cases they should be designed with detailing and materials to withstand corrosion and vandalism.

MODULAR SHELTERS

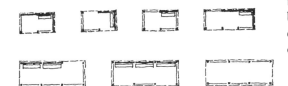

A modular system should be designed for flexibility of location, capacity, planning or fixing arrangement. Modules may be dictated by variations on fixed seating arrangements, clear or solid sides requirements, freestanding or cantilevered structural options.

COORDINATION

Shelters should either respond to the surrounding architectural qualities or be part of an overall street furniture theme. Shelters may become an extension of and compliment to the lighting and signage supports. Lighting incorporated in shelters should be integral and vandal-proof.

Facilities for advertising or information may be included which might actually fund the provision and maintenance of shelters.

CANOPIES

FUNCTION

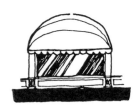

Canopies are either fixed to buildings or freestanding providing shelter from the elements. Canopies may provide a highly decorative and colourful quality to a streetscape.

They may be particularly valuable in city locations where exceptional winds are provoked by high buildings making conditions on adjacent pavements intolerable.

Canopies can be temporary or permanent. A 'knock-down' system could be appropriate for one-day market structures.

GENERAL PRINCIPLES

STRUCTURES

FUNCTION

A structure may or may not provide protection from the weather. It may serve the following functions:

- Create a sense of place.
- Act as a linking element.
- Form gateways.
- Signal specific nodes or points of activity.

Commonly these may take the form of bandstands, rostra, stages, pavilions, gazebos, festival structures, information kiosks, telephone kiosks, public toilets, entrances to underground facilities, exhibition structures, and coverings for outdoor concerts, stadia and pools.

Each of these different forms will have their own particular set of requirements which should be investigated thoroughly. Requirements may include:

- Lighting
- Drainage
- Access
- Signage
- Seating
- Audio/visual
- Heating/ventilation
- Security
- Specialist equipment
- Particular maintenance

OPEN STRUCTURES

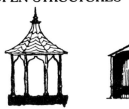

Arbours, trellises, and pergolas may be incorporated into parks, gardens and housing developments to support climbing plant material. Timber and steel are the most common construction materials.

TENSILE STRUCTURES

ELEVATION

Tensile structures often take on a tent-like form constructed in dynamic parabolic shapes. They are formed of lightweight fabrics supported on pylons, poles or arches and secured with tensioned steel cables. They may have open or closed side coverings providing relatively uninterrupted floor space for the area covered.

PNEUMATIC STRUCTURES

Based on stabilisation by positive internal air pressure, these structures form simple but highly technical constructions. Their scale, forms and uses are diverse. The only permanent feature required is a regular kerb against which the margins of the inflated structure can fit.

STABILITY

All structures should be stable in high winds and be capable of withstanding snow loading or temperature fluctuations dependant on location.

FIXING

Fixing details vary according to the permanency of the structure:

- Permanent constructions may require concrete foundations.
- Temporary constructions may only require steel pegs, earth anchors, deadweight anchors in lawn areas, or expansion bolts for fixing on to hard paved areas.

FABRIC COVERINGS

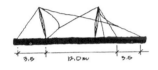

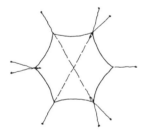

Materials or textiles should be:

- Resistant to the low and high temperature differentials, for instance −25°C to +75°C in Europe.
- Fire resistant.
- Waterproof.
- Corrosion resistant.
- Balanced in tensile and tearing strength in the warp and weft.
- Resistant to rubbing and chafing.

Fabrics most commonly used are canvas and PVC coated polyester.

Fabrics may be single or double skinned. The multi-sheet structure provides a higher degree of insulation and may be capable of forming a permanent covering.

GENERAL PRINCIPLES

IIDABASHI · TOKYO · JAPAN
· SOLID CONTEMPORARY DESIGN FOR
  A DOUBLE PHONE KIOSK
· WOULD SUIT A HISTORIC OR MODERN
  CONTEXT
· CAST ALUMINIUM

HIMEJI · JAPAN
· TELEPHONE KIOSK WITH SIMPLE
  NEAT DETAILING
· A HINT OF TRADITION IN THE
  ROOF PITCH

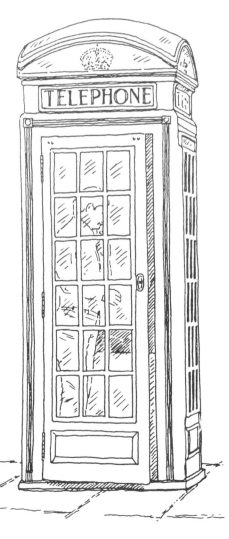

LONDON · UK
· CLASSIC 'K2' LISTED PHONE BOX
· CAST IRON PAINTED PILLAR BOX
  RED IN ORDER TO BE CONSPICUOUS
· PERFORATED CROWN MOTIF ACTS AS
  VENTILATION

MOULINS , FRANCE
, TRANSPARENT PHONE KIOSK DOES
NOT COMPETE WITH SURROUNDING
ARCHITECTURE
, TRIPLE BOOTH IN ONE
, NOTE DOOR HANDLE DESIGN

PIONEER SQUARE · SEATTLE · USA
· CAST ALUMINIUM PHONE HOUSINGS
· NO PROTECTION FOR THE USER BUT
  WELL DESIGNED PIECES OF STREET
  FURNITURE

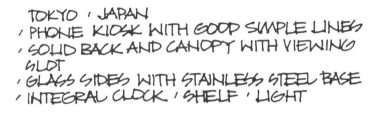

TOKYO · JAPAN
· PHONE KIOSK WITH GOOD SIMPLE LINES
· SOLID BACK AND CANOPY WITH VIEWING
  SLOT
· GLASS SIDES WITH STAINLESS STEEL BASE
· INTEGRAL CLOCK · SHELF · LIGHT

DALLAS · TEXAS · USA
· CYLINDRICAL PHONE BOOTHS
· GROUPED IN THREES
· NEAT TUBULAR CONCEPT

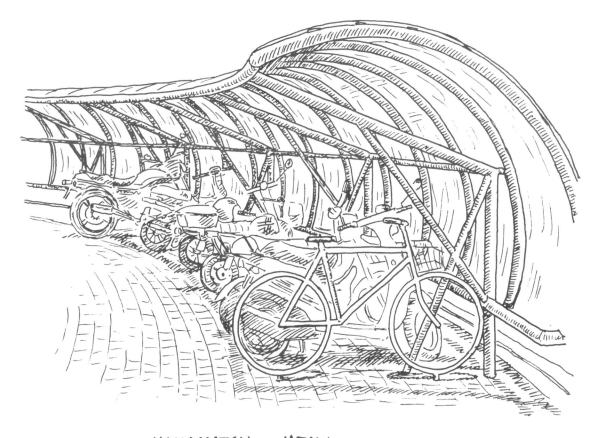

HAMAMATSU · JAPAN
, BIKE SHELTER
, STEEL STRUCTURE PAINTED BROWN
, STAINLESS STEEL FIXED BIKE LIKE
  END REPLACES THE NEED FOR
  SIGNAGE

TSUKUBA CENTRE · JAPAN
· BUS STOP AND TERMINAL
· CONCRETE SUPPORT WITH STEEL
  FRAME AND CANTILEVERED
  CURVED ROOF

LORING GREENWAY · MINNEAPOLIS
· HEAVY TIMBER STRUCTURE TO
  SHADE SEATING AREA
· INTIMATE SPOT CREATED WITH THE
  IMPRESSION OF A ROOF

VIENNA / AUSTRIA
/ STAINLESS STEEL STRUCTURE
  LOCATED IN THE HISTORIC CENTRE
/ BASES INCORPORATE PLANTING
  SUPPORTS

COLUMBUS PARK / BOSTON / USA
/ VAULTED TIMBER STRUCTURE ON
  CONCRETE COLUMNS
/ DEFINES PERIMETER PROMENADE

GENERAL PRINCIPLES

NICOLLET MALL · MINNEAPOLIS · USA
· BUS SHELTER DESIGNED AS A SOLID
PIECE OF STREET ARCHITECTURE
· SIDES INCORPORATE STORAGE AND
INFORMATION BOARDS

KYOTO / JAPAN
BUS SHELTER WITH CANTILEVERED STEEL
STRUCTURE AND STRETCHED CANVAS AWNING

CHAING MAI , THAILAND
· BUS SHELTER WITH TYPICAL THAI
ARCHITECTURAL DETAILING

HAWAII
· SIMPLE TWO POLE STRUCTURE
WITH ROOF AND BENCH SUSPENDED
· CEDAR SHINGLE ROOF

THAILAND
′ BUS SHELTER ON STILTS OVER
DRAINAGE CHANNEL
′ ACCESS VIA TIMBER BRIDGE

BALTIMORE HARBOR PLACE ′ USA
′ HEAVY TIMBER BRIDGE STRUCTURE
′ LIGHT WEIGHT 'FLYING' CANOPY WITH
TUBULAR STEEL AND TENSIONED CABLES

COURT PAVILION OF THE CITY RAILWAY , VIENNA
, RICHLY DECORATED CANOPY
, FIXINGS BETWEEN STRUCTURE AND STONE PLINTH
EXPRESSED AND ELEGANTLY DETAILED

RIVER WIEN BUILDINGS , VIENNA
, A BOLD COMPOSITION OF PAVILIONS , GATEWAYS ,
TRELLIS AND SCREENS BUILT IN STONE
, PLANTING IS INCORPORATED POSITIVELY AS AN
ARCHITECTURAL ELEMENT

GENERAL PRINCIPLES

· HONG KONG
· SHADE GIVING STRUCTURE IN A COMPLEX
  OF HIGH RISE APARTMENTS
· CONTRAST OF FAMILIAR TRADITIONAL
  DETAILING WITH FEATURELESS TOWERS
· A REAL OASIS

OCEAN PARK / HONG KONG
· ROLLING WAVE LIKE PROFILED
STEEL ROOF OVER QUEUING
AREA

OCEAN PARK / HONG KONG
· GRP ENTRANCE KIOSK
· YELLOW WITH BLUE SEA HORSE LOGO

SEATTLE / WASHINGTON / USA
· TRAM STOP SHELTER
· STRAIGHT FORWARD STEEL
STRUCTURE WITH ADD ON ROOF
SIGNAGE FOR A MORE ELABORATE
SILHOUETTE

174   GENERAL PRINCIPLES

Water Features
Drinking Fountains
Hydrants

Water Features
Drinking Fountains
Hydrants

WATER FEATURES

DESIGN CONSIDERATIONS

The following aspects of water feature design should be considered:

- Movement.
- Noise (white sound).
- Cooling effect.
- Reflections.
- Overshadowing.

MOVEMENT

Moving water will catch the light and sparkle. Calm or moving water can create very different atmospheres:

- Tranquility
- Activity

WIND

Wind deflection should be considered when locating jets or designing falling water. In urban areas, in particular, it may be necessary to install a wind vane and sensor to monitor wind speed and direction, and to regulate jet heights.

NOZZLES

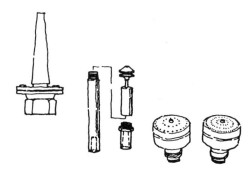

In windy locations selection of the appropriate nozzle may help to reduce splash. There are two basic types of nozzles:

- *Smooth bore*: funnel-shaped, narrowing towards the top to increase the water velocity, producing thin high jets.

- *Formed*: many different shapes are available to create different configurations of sheet water, low domed and fan sheets of water are generally less susceptible to wind deflection.

Spray heads for large fountains are usually formed by a number of nozzles clustered together. For smaller fountains a shower head type of attachment may be sufficient.

HYDRAULICS

The principles of turbulent and laminar flow form the basis of any fountain design. Flow conditions may be altered by:

176

- Increasing or decreasing water velocity by altering channel widths or gradients.
- Altering the depths of basins.
- Adjusting the design of any lips.
- Increasing or decreasing the drag force by a change of material.
- Adjusting water pressure.

LOCATION AND DESIGN

Water features in cities can create a cooling effect in hot, hard paved areas. Where possible water features should be located in the sun so that the sparkling qualities of water are exploited.

If the water feature is designed to reflect, it should be located in the shade, or with a dark-coloured pool base.

The container or pool should generally look brimful to give the impression of abundance. Overhanging edges create a shadow line which helps to conceal the scum line.

HARDWARE

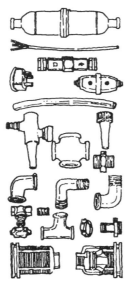

The essential components which should be considered in any fountain design are:

- Lighting.
- Inlets.
- Overflows.
- Water level sensor.
- Filters.

These should all be integrated elements to minimise vandalism.

MANAGEMENT

All water features should have an efficient filter system. An uneven or dark-coloured pool bottom will help to camouflage dirt. Management techniques may also include the incorporation of a water treatment plant for large fountains, oxygenating aquatic planting for informal natural features, and stocking fish to maintain algae-free water in lakes and untreated pools.

SAFETY

Margins of water features should be well defined for the safety of children, and deep pools should be avoided in civic areas.

DRINKING FOUNTAINS

MATERIALS

Materials should be coordinated with bollards, litter bins, and structures.

LOCATION

Siting should be out of the mainstream of pedestrian traffic. They should be easy to use and accessible by handicapped persons.

SELECTION

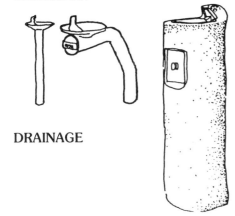

A unit should be selected which is:

- Workable by handicapped persons.
- Easy for children to use.
- Designed with a protected nozzle for hygiene.

DRAINAGE

Drainage may be either through the unit or by overflow into an adjacent gully or soakaway.

CLEANSING

A drinking fountain unit may incorporate other facilities for washing hands, clothes, or utensils. Any non-potable water should be clearly identified.

HYDRANTS

LOCATION OF FIRE HYDRANTS

Hydrants should be flush wall-mounted or underground to avoid clutter and obstruction, but easily accessible and visible for emergency use.

IRRIGATION SYSTEMS

Irrigation systems should be as inconspicuous as possible to mimimise vandalism. They may be manual, semi-automatic or fully automatic dependant on budget, water availability and management regimes. Local regulations governed by water authorities may dictate their design and position, and may impose a licence for certain volumes of extraction only.

FOUNTAIN OF LOVE · CLIVEDEN · ENGLAND
· FOCUS AT THE END OF A LONG GRAND AVENUE
· ENORMOUS STONE SHELL WITH
TRICKLING WATER

CHRISTIAN SCIENCE CENTER, BOSTON
, CONCEALED NOZZLES SET IN PAIRS OF
CROSSING JETS
, PAVING CONTINUITY MAINTAINED

DALLAS , USA
, COURTYARD WATER FEATURE
, A WALL OF WATER
, GRANITE CENTRAL STONE WITH BUBBLER FOUNTAIN
, GRANITE SEAT HEIGHT POOL EDGE

LES HALLES · PARIS · FRANCE
· LONG TROUGH WITH A SERIES
  OF SPOUTS
· STONE SEAT HEIGHT EDGING

COBBLERS SQUARE · CHICAGO
· WATER CHANNEL CUT THROUGH
  COBBLE PAVING
· IN SITU CONCRETE BLOCKS FOR
  SEATING

IIDABASHI · TOKYO · JAPAN
· URBAN WATER COURSE DETAILED
  SENSITIVELY WITH BRIDGES AND
  TERRACED PAVING

DALLAS , USA
, SERIES OF STONE DISHES IN STONE SURROUND
, WALL WHITE WASHED WITH STONE COPING
, SIMPLE AND TRANQUIL

CLIVEDEN , ENGLAND
, THREE SIDED GARDEN FOUNTAIN
TERMINATING A STONE BALUSTRADE

CHRISTIAN SCIENCE CENTER / BOSTON
· ENORMOUS RECTANGULAR REFLECTING
  POOL WITH A POLISHED GRANITE LIP
· WATER SLIPS EVENLY OVER LIP INTO A
  CONCEALED CHANNEL FOR RECIRCULATION

LEVIS STRAUSS / EMBARCADERO /
SAN FRANCISCO / USA
· WATER FALLS OVER CONCRETE BLOCKS
· PLANTING AND STEP SEATING
  INTEGRATED INTO DESIGN

DALLAS · TEXAS · USA
· AN UNCOMPLICATED AND APPROPRIATE
FOUNTAIN DESIGN RESPONDING TO THE
CLEAN LINES OF THE SURROUNDING
ARCHITECTURE

WILLIAMS SQUARE · LAS COLINAS · USA
· SCULPTURES OF LARGER THAN LIFE
  MUSTANGS GALLOP THROUGH WATER
· SMALL SPRAY FOUNTAINS CREATE
  A DYNAMIC EFFECT

AMALFI · ITALY
· SMALL MOSSY FIGURATIVE FOUNTAIN
  WITH WATER BUBBLING OVER UMBRELLA

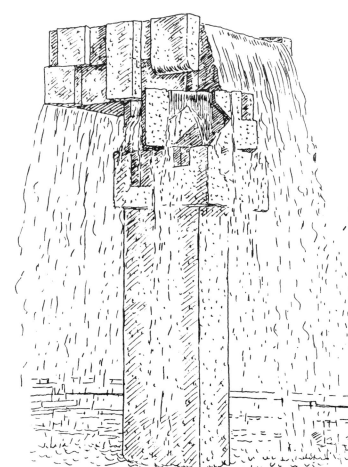

TSUKUBA SCIENCE CITY · JAPAN
· VERTICAL SCULPTURAL FORM
  WITH WATER GUSHING OVER
  INTO A LARGE POOL TO CONTAIN
  THE SPLASH

FREEWAY PARK ' SEATTLE ' USA
' DRAMATIC WATER FALL OVER HIGH LEDGES OF
OFF SHUTTER CONCRETE
' IMPRESSION OF A MOUNTAIN STREAM CASCADE

THE REGENT HOTEL ' HONG KONG
' FIBREGLASS 'STONE' WALL AS A
BACKDROP TO CASCADES OF WATER
' A POOL AND PLANTING AT THE BASE
' IMPRESSIVE SCALE

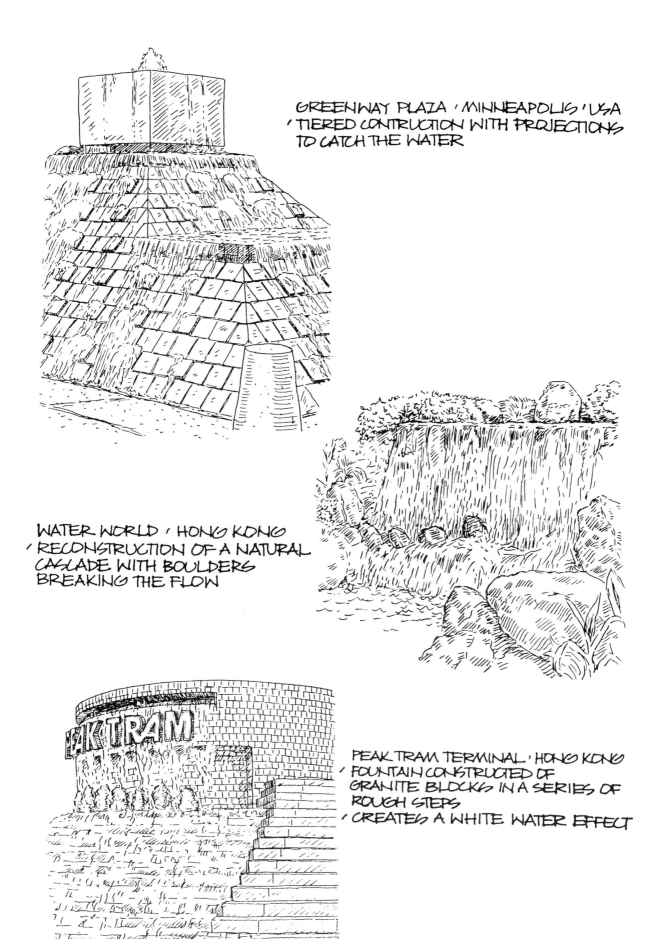

GREENWAY PLAZA · MINNEAPOLIS · USA
· TIERED CONTRUCTION WITH PROJECTIONS
TO CATCH THE WATER

WATER WORLD · HONG KONG
· RECONSTRUCTION OF A NATURAL
CASCADE WITH BOULDERS
BREAKING THE FLOW

PEAK TRAM TERMINAL · HONG KONG
· FOUNTAIN CONSTRUCTED OF
GRANITE BLOCKS IN A SERIES OF
ROUGH STEPS
· CREATES A WHITE WATER EFFECT

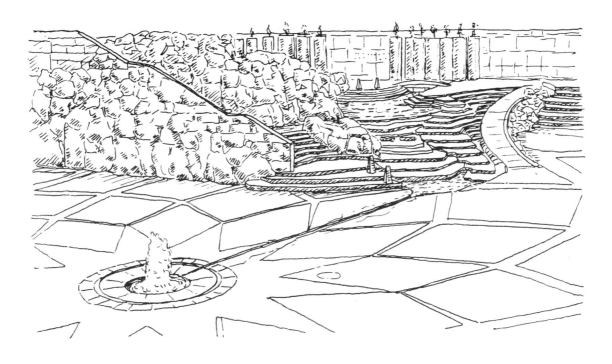

TSUKUBA CENTRE · NEAR TOKYO · JAPAN
· WATER TERRACES EMERGE FROM A MOUNTAIN
OF ROUGH HEWN BOULDERS
· CHANNEL SLICES THROUGH PAVING AND
THE FEATURE TERMINATES IN A BUBBLE JET

NATURAL HISTORY MUSEUM · CAPE TOWN
· SECTION OF WATER FEATURE
· BRONZE LIP WITH CASCADING WATER

LEVIS STRAUSS · SAN FRANCISCO
· ENORMOUS ROUGH HEWN LUMP
OF STONE AS THE CENTREPIECE
· STEPPING STONE ACCESS TO ALL
PARTS OF THE FOUNTAIN

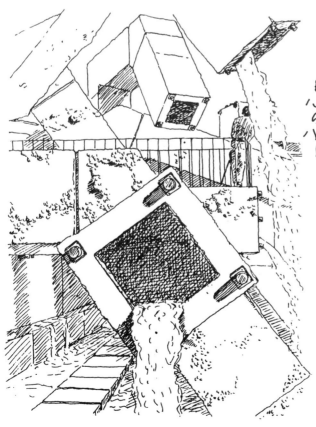

EMBARCADERO · SAN FRANCISCO
· JUMBLE OF MASSIVE HOLLOW ARMS
SOME GUSHING WATER
· VIEWING PLATFORM LOCATED
WITHIN THE WATER FEATURE

PIONEER SQUARE · SEATTLE · USA
· CONTINUOUSLY FLOWING FOUNTAIN /
DRINKING OR CLEANSING FOUNTAIN
· BRASS SPOUT FIXED TO A CONCRETE
BASE

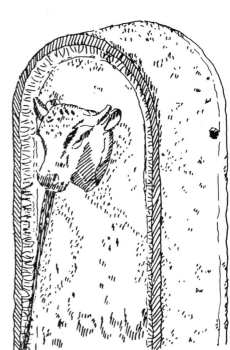

TURIN · ITALY
· UPPER PORTION OF CAST IRON DRINKING /
CLEANSING FOUNTAIN

TSUKUBA SCIENCE CITY · JAPAN
· ELEGANT STAINLESS STEEL DRINKING
FOUNTAIN WITH TAP
· LARGE GRANITE DRAINAGE GULLY
· DESIGNED FOR WHEELCHAIR AND
CHILDREN USE

GENERAL PRINCIPLES

TOKYO , JAPAN
, DRINKING FOUNTAIN IN STONE
, STEP FOR CHILDREN WITH TOE RECESS

TOKYO , JAPAN
, CONCRETE DRINKING FOUNTAIN
WITH STEP FOR CHILDREN AND
SIDE DRAINAGE SLOT

TSUKUBA SCIENCE CITY , JAPAN
, CANTILEVERED GRANITE FOUNTAIN
, REFLECTIVE SHEET SUPPORT WITH
COUNTER WEIGHT AND DRAIN ON THE
OPPOSITE SIDE

KIYOMIZU · KYOTO · JAPAN
· WATER FALLS FROM ELEVATED CHANNELS
  TO A PRECISE SPOT IN A POOL BELOW
· STEPPING STONES LEAD YOU TO THE
  FALLS FOR CLEANSING

GINKAKUJI · KYOTO · JAPAN
· CLEANSING WATER IN A STONE CONTAINER
  AT THE TEMPLE ENTRANCE
· A MINI ROOF CONSTRUCTION PROTECTS THE
  WATER FROM CONTAMINATION

Section 3

A COORDINATED APPROACH

PREFACE TO SECTION 3

The concept of developing a coordinated system of street furniture was discussed in Section 1. Several examples in which the authors were involved together in South Africa are illustrated in the next few pages. This work is still evolving and responding to cultural and environmental influences, as well as the specific needs of each project. It is these very influences which have in the end created the richness and variety of examples from many places around the world, captured in Section 2.

These few examples represent an evolution in design thinking. The process started with the development of a street furniture manual for Durban.

Durban

DURBAN MANUAL PROVIDES THE PROTOTYPE

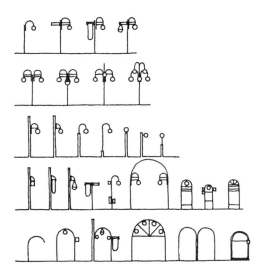

The concept for this project was to create a 'vocabulary' of components, or a kit of parts, with which other designers or the city departments could create their own variations on a theme.

The components basically consisted of a 90 mm diameter tubular steel pole, to which various other street furniture elements could be clamped by means of a standard fixing collar. This allowed the many city departments to share a common type of support pole on which to fix their lighting, street names, traffic signage, litter bins and other elements. Additional street furniture elements, such as telephone kiosks, benches, balustrades and tree guards were limited to a 30 mm, 60 mm and 90 mm diameter tubing.

The system has been implemented over the last few years in several precincts of the city, including the historic centre, the exposition site and the beachfront. In cases where architects in the private sector are commissioned to work on public projects, they are usually provided with a copy of the street furniture manual, and are requested to fit in with the overall theme.

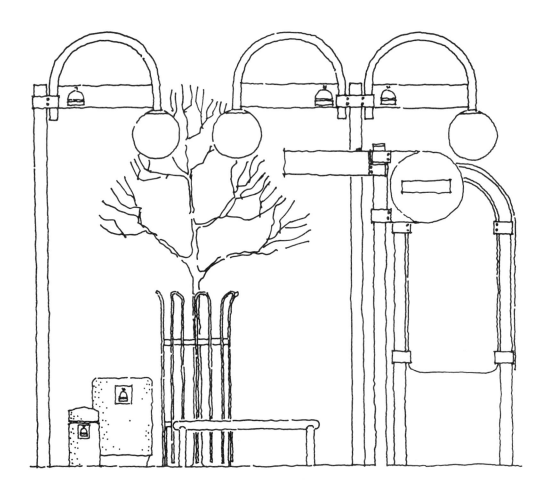

196   A COORDINATED APPROACH

CHURCH STREET · DURBAN
· SITING OF ALL ELEMENTS IN RELATION
TO EACH OTHER AND SURROUNDING
ARCHITECTURE WAS AN IMPORTANT PART
OF THE PROJECT

ALBANY GROVE · DURBAN
· STREET NAME AND TRAFFIC SIGNAGE
MOUNTED ON ONE POLE
· CITY LOGO 'CUT OUT' GIVES A SENSE
OF LOCATION

Woodbridge Island

A WOOD THEME FOR WOODBRIDGE ISLAND

In parallel to the tubular metal examples, several timber themes have been developed, three of which are illustrated here. Timber was chosen, not only because of the corrosive conditions at the coast, but also for its informal character, especially in residential and recreational areas.

At Woodbridge Island, a residential development near Cape Town, a hardwood was used for the lamp-posts and signage, while old railway sleepers were recycled for use as bollards, benches and footbridges.

The timber design is reflected in the treatment of the railings on the bridge over the lagoon, and was originally intended to respond to the verandah handrails of the houses. The timber theme was derived from the early wooden bridge which still stands, the idea finding expression even in the detailed graphics of the street name boards.

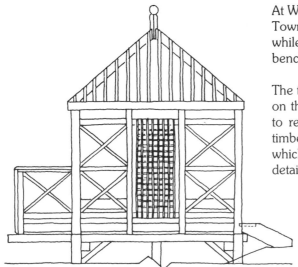

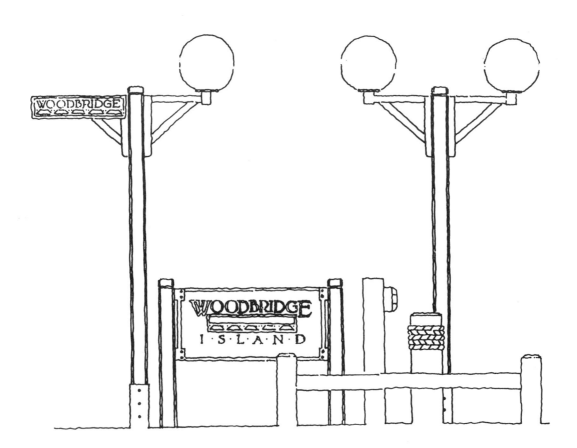

A COORDINATED APPROACH

WOODBRIDGE ISLAND
· TIMBER GAZEBO SITS OVER THE WATER
AND FRAMES VIEWS OF THE LAGOON

WOODBRIDGE ISLAND
· NEW CONCRETE ROAD BRIDGE 'SOFTENED'
WITH TIMBER BALUSTRADING

Longmarket Mall

DECORATIVE VARIATIONS FOR LONGMARKET MALL

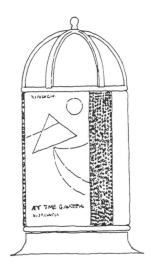

Built in 1985 and one of the early pedestrian projects in Cape Town, this short mall has its own distinctive character, in keeping with the historic City Hall on one side and a modern office block on the other.

Although a tubular steel theme was adopted for the lamp-posts and benches, a more decorative effect was created by using perforated metal bands for the light fittings to create a soft sparkling effect and at the same time reduce the glare from the high-pressure sodium lamps. A similar material was used for the seats and litter bins. Individual seats were designed in preference to benches, to discourage them from being used for sleeping by tramps.

The decorative metalwork is painted a red ochre colour, and contrasts against the bold and simple cobbled paving and the grey bush-hammered concrete of an associated fountain feature. Some of the details are intentionally reminiscent of the older Victorian elements found in the city.

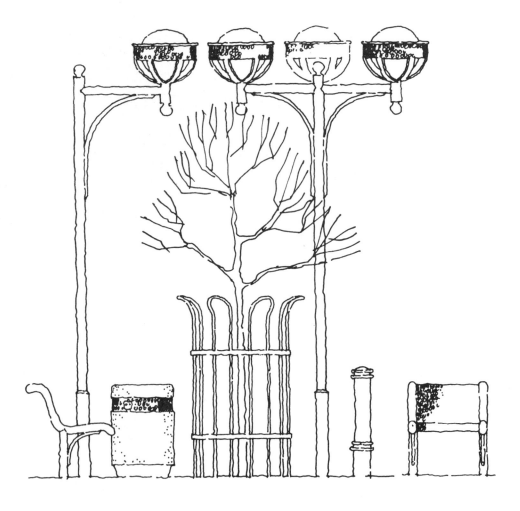

A COORDINATED APPROACH

LONGMARKET MALL
- REFLECTION OF CITY HALL WITH A TYPICAL GROUP OF STREET FURNITURE
- BUSH HAMMERED CONCRETE BIN RELATES TO GRANITE AND COBBLED PAVING

LONGMARKET MALL
- ENTRANCE TO MALL IS EMPHASISED WITH A CLUSTER OF LUMINAIRES

LONGMARKET MALL
- PERFORATED STEEL SEATING MATERIAL CASTS A DECORATIVE SHADOW
- INTERLOCKING FANS OF COBBLES ARE EDGED WITH OLD GRANITE KERBS

Victoria & Alfred Waterfront

WATERFRONT REVIVAL

The old Victoria and Alfred harbour front in Cape Town is being revived as a major tourist destination. The street furniture theme here attempts to provide a thread between the old and the new, the working harbour and the tourist shops, the naval alongside the merchant shipping and re-creation boating.

The robust and corrosive maritime environment led to a combined use of hardwood, cast iron, stainless steel and concrete in the design of the streetscape. Many of the elements reflect a nautical influence. The sturdy style of the street furniture is matched by the paving which consists of brushed concrete, cobbles and a dark brick, and by the heavy concrete bollards which are used in combination with chains.

A COORDINATED APPROACH

VICTORIA AND ALFRED WATERFRONT
- 'CANNON' BALL BOLLARDS IN
EXPOSED AGGREGATE CONCRETE
FINISH

VICTORIA AND ALFRED WATERFRONT
- RAILINGS WITH TIMBER POSTS
- STEEL RAILS AND CAST IRON BALLS

VICTORIA AND ALFRED WATERFRONT
- LAMP STANDARDS WITH AN ARM TO
TAKE A BANNER.
- DETAILING RESPONDS TO HISTORIC
MARITIME CONTEXT

Mdantsane

SELF-HELP STREET FURNITURE FOR MDANTSANE

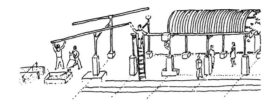

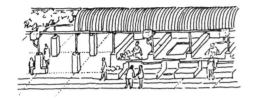

The streetscape design of the commercial centre formed part of a larger upgrading project for a residential township near East London, Ciskei.

The proposals include a system of pedestrian walkway structures, used to define urban spaces, provide weather protection and also to serve as market stalls. It was seen as an additive system which could start merely as an open frame, but which could be later filled. The structure is used in conjunction with low cement-block walls and piers, which are also locally manufactured. Seating, gateways and bus shelters are designed to be integral with the structure which performs a particularly useful function while newly planted trees become established.

Emphasis was placed on locally available materials and local unskilled labour, a scaffold structure being easy and quick to erect, and which in turn would become a support for lighting, signs, banners and litter bins, as well as awnings and creepers.

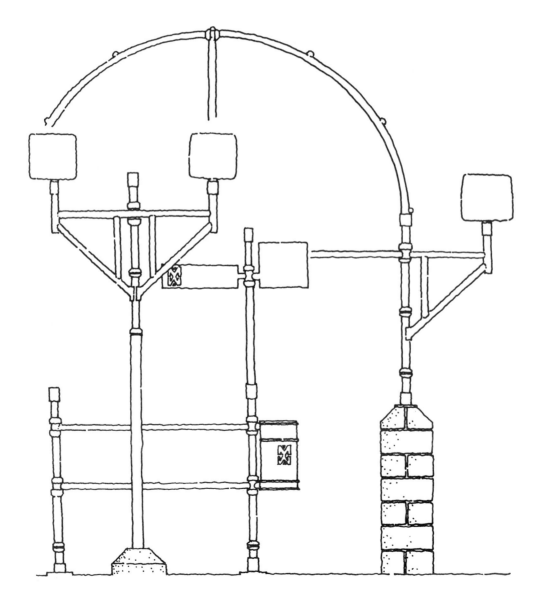

COMMERCIAL CENTRE · MDANTSANE · CISKEI
' EXISTING TYPICAL STREET SCENE
' NO PROVISION FOR FRUIT SELLERS
' OVERSCALED AND VISUALLY IMPOSING
  ADVERTISING TECHNIQUES AND LITTLE
  SENSE OF PLACE.

St George's Street

A PEDESTRIAN NETWORK FOR CAPE TOWN

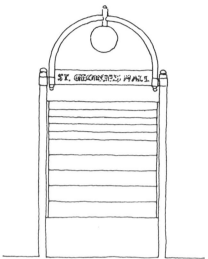

The idea of the standard diameter pole and fixing collar was carried further in the pedestrian malls of Cape Town. Greater articulation was introduced into the design of the poles, bollards and light fittings to ackowledge the historic centre of the city while reflecting the modernity of the St George's Street precinct.

The designers made a survey of the older Victorian cast iron elements, such as lamps, bollards, railings and benches, to ensure some continuity between old and new, and to strengthen the 'sense of place'. This particular theme is being used throughout the central business district as each section of the overall pedestrian project is implemented. An attempt has been made however, to allow each individual street or project to have its own distinctive detailing, as with the Longmarket Mall example.

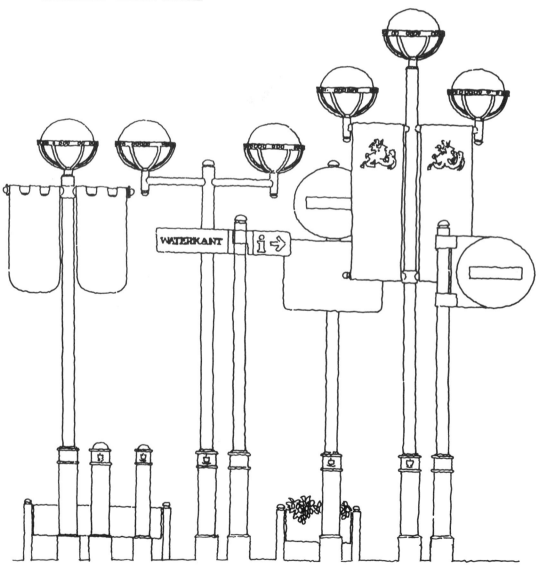

206   A COORDINATED APPROACH

THIBAULT SQUARE TERMINATES ST GEORGE'S MALL
- STEEL MESH BENCH WITH INDIVIDUAL ARM RESTS
- MOUNTED ON LOW PLANTER WALL

ST GEORGE'S MALL
- KIOSK, STREET LAMP AND BENCHES
- INDIVIDUAL LUMINAIRES MOUNTED ONTO
  KIOSK STRUCTURE

King's Beach

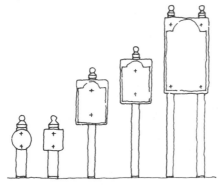

The upgrading of the Port Elizabeth beachfront, introducing new beach resort amenities, gave the opportunity to develop a site furniture theme that reflected both the holiday atmosphere and the Victorian traditions of the older parts of the city.

A decorative lattice-work is proposed for litter bins and fences, and this theme is carried over into the shade structures and kiosk buidings of the beachfront. The timber is painted a sparkling white to give a sense of lightness against the dark facebrick of the buildings. Cast aluminium, cast iron and stainless steel have also been recommended for other furniture fittings to minimise problems of corrosion at the coast.

Bibliography

The American Society of Landscape Architects Foundation, The US Department of Housing and Urban Development (1975) *Barrier Free Site Design*. Government Printing Office, Washington DC.

Boeminghaus, Dieter (1982) *Pedestrian Areas and Design Elements*. Karl Kramer Verlag, Stuttgart.

Breines, S. & Dean, William J. (1974) *The Pedestrian Revolution, Streets without Cars*. Vintage Books, New York.

Department of the Environment, Welsh Office (1973) *The Design of Streets and Other Space*. HMSO, London.

Design Council in association with the Royal Town Planning Institute (1979) *Streets Ahead*. Design Council, London.

Design Council (1976) *Street Scene*. Design Council, London.

Durban Corporation (1986) *Durban Street Furniture Manual*. Unpublished manual prepared by Oberholzer van Papendorp, Landscape Architects.

Cartwright, Richard M. (1980) *Design of Urban Spaces*. Architectural Press, London.

Follis, John & Hammer, Dave (1979) *Architectural Signage and Graphics*. Whitney Library of Design, an imprint of Watson-Guptill Publications, New York.

Halprin, Lawrence (1972) *Cities*. MIT Press, Cambridge, Mass.

Harnaford and Partners (1977) *Rundle Mall, Design and Implementation Report*. D. J. Woolman, South Australia.

Ramanti, Raquel (1981) *How to Save Your Own Street*. Dolphin Books, New York.

Shepheard, Peter (1969) *Gardens*. MacDonald and Co in association with the Council for Industrial Design, London.

Tandy, C. (1972) *Handbook of Urban Landscape*. Architects Journal, London.

Walker, Theodore, D. (1978) *Site Design and Construction Detailing*. PDA Publishers, Indiana.

Weddle, A. E. (1967) *Techniques of Landscape Architecture*. Heinemann, London.

Index

of places illustrated in Section 2